Rediscovering
YOU

ROSA JONES, LPC

Rediscovering YOU

An Active Spiritual Journey to Embracing Your Most Authentic Self

XULON PRESS

Xulon Press
555 Winderley Pl, Suite 225
Maitland, FL 32751
407.339.4217
www.xulonpress.com

© 2024 by Rosa Jones, LPC

All rights reserved solely by the author. The author guarantees all contents are original and do not infringe upon the legal rights of any other person or work. No part of this book may be reproduced in any form without the permission of the author.

Due to the changing nature of the Internet, if there are any web addresses, links, or URLs included in this manuscript, these may have been altered and may no longer be accessible. The views and opinions shared in this book belong solely to the author and do not necessarily reflect those of the publisher. The publisher therefore disclaims responsibility for the views or opinions expressed within the work.

Unless otherwise indicated, Scripture quotations taken from the Holy Bible, New Living Translation (NLT). Copyright ©1996, 2004, 2007 by Tyndale House Foundation. Used by permission of Tyndale House Publishers, Inc.

Paperback ISBN-13: 978-1-66289-482-4
Hard Cover ISBN-13: 978-1-66289-483-1
Ebook ISBN-13: 978-1-66289-484-8

Table of Contents

Acknowledgements................................vii
Introduction.................................... ix

Chapter 1: **Understanding Confidence**.....................1

Chapter 2: **Defining Healthy Self-Esteem**..................13

Chapter 3: **Valuing Yourself**..............................27

Chapter 4: **Embracing Your Strength**......................51

Chapter 5: **Embracing Your Weakness**.....................65

Chapter 6: **Valuing Others**..............................101

Chapter 7: **The Journey Ahead**...........................113

Acknowledgements

With special thanks:

To my incredible husband, Jefferson Jones, who loves, supports and appreciates me like no one else.

To my two sons, Peter & Abraham, who bring me so much joy, contentment & hope for the future.

To my mother, Doncella Bell, who provided me with a firm foundation of faith.

To my mentor, Dedra Anderson, for discipling me and my family.

To my sister-friends, Kelly, Lynette, Stephanie, Linna, Christy, & Juniece, who pray for me and encourage me to chase my dreams.

To my clients, mentees, & students, whose stories and courage keep hope & healing flowing through my life. Thank you for choosing me to walk with you.

Introduction

Before fourth grade, I considered myself to be a kid who was energetic but somewhat timid and shy, especially in new situations. My dad was a functional addict, so we moved around a lot in those early years. I attended five different schools before finishing elementary school. Looking back, I realize that my timidity was not my natural way of relating to the world, it was a byproduct of a constant feeling of anxiety. I worried about whether or not my dad was coming home, whether there would be enough food for all of us to eat, whether mom could afford to put gas in the car to get us to school, and what my friends would think if they came over and saw a living room with no furniture and roaches crawling on the walls. That's a lot of worry for a kid. It was exhausting.

Once my parents were divorced and most of those fears dissolved, my real self began to emerge. I started raising my hand to answer questions in class, ran for club offices, auditioned for the softball team (even though I sucked), and started my own club. I made friends with kids that were invisible to other people, entered writing contests, and dazzled the fans as a cheerleader at games and competitions. Well, what do you know, I was naturally confident after all!!!

That feeling of confidence allowed me to create an enjoyable experience for myself in high school, helped me to excel academically and socially in college, helped me earn two advanced degrees by the age of 27, and helped me launch a successful and vibrant career.

However, somewhere along the way I noticed I was stuck. Shortly after I had my children in my early 30's, I felt a shift. I had goals, dreams, and plans that I wanted to fulfill but I really struggled to forge a path forward. Did I lose my confidence? After much thought, prayer, and contemplation I realized that a lack of confidence was not my problem. **I was stuck.**

What I discovered is that I was not fully committed to the belief that I truly deserved all of the happiness and contentment that change could bring. I didn't value my authentic self enough to take the types of risk I needed to take and I didn't really trust myself. I half-heartedly trusted God and I saw my limitations as a major threat to my success. I wasn't just stuck, **I was trapped.** But God, in all of His goodness, did not leave me there. With the strength and wisdom available to me at the time, I had enough sense to press beyond my discomfort, partner with God, and move forward while still being deathly afraid.

That's something that people don't tell us. Many times you will have to do things even when you're scared. If you waited until all of the fear fell off of you, you would never get anywhere! Some people you see in the places and spaces you long to be did not get there because they were super bold and confident. Some of them fought their way through fear, doubt, shame, negative self-talk, doubters, haters, and self-sabotage. The beauty of a complicated journey is that you become better along the way. The process shapes you, changes you, fortifies you, and builds you up. There are so many great treasures the Lord deposits in you in the process. But you will never become better if you aren't able to do some things scared. Say Amen and let me get us back on track!!!

With the Lord's help, I spent the rest of my 30's learning bit by bit how to keep moving forward no matter how I felt about my situation or circumstances. I grew in faith. I also learned how to really, truly value myself as a woman created in the image of God. Not just by embracing the things about me that I was proud of and liked to show off, but by loving the unlovable parts of me: my anger, lust, and pride. I learned to accept all of myself just like Jesus accepts all of me. Doing so has helped me approach painful parts of myself instead of avoiding them. And just like that, the Lord paved pathways that allowed healing and restoration to flow into my soul. These were deeply dark and broken places that were hidden to me and longing for the love of Jesus. I began walking in levels of healing I never knew I needed! I received healing in areas of my life that I didn't believe healing was possible.

As a professional counselor, pastor, and coach, I work with people from so many backgrounds: challenging children, defiant teenagers, curious coeds, driven executives, exhausted pastors, and spiritual leaders. Here is what I have noticed. No matter how smart or successful a person is, the key to breakthrough lies in attending to one's inner life, one's thoughts, emotions, beliefs, and fears. Building a healthy self-esteem plus tending to your inner life is a pathway to healing. **When you invite Jesus into your journey of self-awareness, discovery, and love, freedom and breakthrough are inevitable.**

It doesn't matter what you've been through or what you're experiencing right now, healing is always possible because of Jesus' work on the cross. It's not a fairytale or some Netflix special. His healing power is real.

That's why I wrote this book. I want you to know that God made you just the way you are. He knows you and He loves you. In John 10:10, Jesus says, *"The thief comes only to steal and kill and destroy. I came that they may have life and have it abundantly"* (ESV). If you want to live an abundant life, you need to follow Christ's example and love yourself well. Your access to abundance is diminished without growing in your capacity to love and accept yourself unconditionally.

Fulfilling God's calling and purpose for your life is so much more than having the confidence to do it. You need to receive the revelation that God made you just the way you are, in all of your beauty and mess, and has a plan to restore you and use you in this Earth for great things. Not just great things for others, but great things for *you* that will bring you joy, peace, and contentment. Can you get with that? Do you want to experience it?

In my 20+ years of helping people heal in schools, churches, and communities, I know this; the way you think about yourself controls everything in your life. **Everything.** *"For as a man thinks in his heart, so is he"* (Prov. 23:7 (NKJ))

God loves you and who you are. His image of you is straight in His heart and mind. He is your maker. We are the ones who need to get our identity straight in our own hearts and minds. This has nothing to do with confidence. Confidence alone will not empower you to fulfill your destiny. You will fulfill your destiny through esteeming yourself properly. The ability to do so provides you with a wholesome filter for all of your thoughts, emotions, and behaviors. Knowing and accepting yourself is a game changer.

So if you are a confident person like me, I challenge you to keep reading. Your confidence does not guard you from a distorted self-image. Stick with me and you will tap into a new level of strength lying right beneath the surface of your heart and mind. To the ones who struggle with confidence, this journey will be pleasantly surprising. You will find yourself stepping forward in ways you never dreamed possible.

Introduction

This book is an ***active*** journey. The pages are filled with teachings that include exercises to help you apply what you are learning to your own life. I encourage you to lean into reflection, contemplation, and introspection. ***There is no growth without self-reflection.***

I also want to encourage you to grow in your ability to think, feel, and trust your Self. Let me be clear, I am *not* talking about being led by your flesh, I am talking about having a healthy enough relationship with your Self that you see yourself, love yourself, and know yourself *without shame*. This type of stability in your relationship with your Self will amplify your ability to see things clearly, make better decisions, and move forward in life despite how you feel. Many believers shy away from self-reflection for fear of doing something outside of God's will, thinking incorrectly, or making a poor choice.

If you find yourself entertaining these types of beliefs, you do not trust your Self and you are controlled by a spirit of fear. *"God has not given you a Spirit of fear, but of love, power, and a sound mind."* (2 Tim. 1:7). Do not allow the enemy to trick you into believing that all you have to do to follow Jesus is to be led by the Spirit. Fear is not always someone balled up in a corner trembling. Sometimes fear also looks like anxiety, avoidance, rejection, confusion, self-sabotage, and lack of productivity. In order to walk with Jesus into abundance (See John 10:10), we must figure some things out in our relationship with our Self.

When we do not trust ourselves, we are not honest with ourselves.
When we are not honest with ourselves, we cannot be honest with God.
When we are not honest with God, we do not trust God.
When we do not trust God, we will struggle to be vulnerable with him.
When we are not able to be vulnerable with God, we will experience lower levels of intimacy with Him.

It is time for women and men of God to learn how to be more open and honest with themselves. Despite popular belief, *God does not want to think or feel for you.* If he wanted to control your thoughts and feelings, he would not have given you a mind or a heart! God does not want to make all of your decisions for you. You are a partner, daughter or son, and co-laborer with the King of the Universe! It is time for you to increase your faith and learn how to use the authority you have been given. If you cannot feel or think freely for yourself, how will you fulfill your calling and bring heaven to earth? Developing a healthier self-esteem is a great place to start.

Let's get to it!

CHAPTER 1
Understanding Confidence

Confidence is a buzzword, especially in circles where there is a major emphasis on leadership. Everyone wants it. Everyone needs it.

Confidence is a state of feeling a particular way. Before we define confidence, I want you to understand that it is not simply a personality or character trait. Are there some people with personalities that tend to be more confident? Absolutely. But confidence has a bit more nuance to it. Confidence is a feeling, and feelings change. It is normal for your feelings to vacillate and for your confidence to change from time to time.

As we begin to learn about confidence, I find this to be a critical piece of information. Some people feel really bad about their struggle with confidence, whether it is an occasional experience or a daily occurance. I pray that this teaching helps to free you from any feelings of guilt or shame associated with wrestling with your confidence. The struggle is normal for all of us, even those of us who are generally confident will have moments and situations in which we question or doubt ourselves and our abilities. Just because you don't see someone struggle doesn't mean they never struggle. Many people fight internal battles with confidence every day and no one ever knows. The mere fact of being human qualifies us for emotional highs and lows. A person who says they don't ever struggle with their confidence is really saying:

"I lack self-awareness."

"I don't want to admit my struggles to you."

"I don't want to share my inner life with you."

Confidence Reflection Questions

1. What are some situations in which you typically feel confident? If you struggle with confidence, list some areas where you have experienced improvement over time.

2. List some areas of your life or situations where you know you lack confidence.

3. When you think about these areas where you struggle, what is your narrative to yourself? How does this struggle make you feel about yourself?

4. Internally, how do you speak to yourself about your confidence struggle?

5. If a close friend confessed to you that they lacked confidence in these same areas, what would you say to encourage them?

6. Compare your response to yourself with your response to a close friend in questions #4 and #5.

    Were you kinder and more gracious with your friend than yourself?

    Yes   No

    If you answered "yes," please attempt to be kinder and more gracious to yourself. Re-write a word of encouragement to yourself below.

7. Remember, how we think about ourselves and what we say to or about our Self *really* matters. What did you discover about yourself through this exercise?

8. Write out a prayer to God about your confidence. You can praise him, make a confession, share your feelings, or ask for help. Don't hold back, He already knows what is going on with you and He wants to support you right where you are.

What is Confidence?

Confidence can be defined as the feeling or belief that one can rely on someone or something; firm trust; the state of being certain about the truth of something; a feeling of self-assurance arising from one's appreciation of one's own abilities or qualities.

Confidence can look like a person in a class or meeting who is actively listening and fully engaged in a lecture or discussion. They look content, while others battle to have their points heard, and they wait patiently and speak with great insight. It's almost like you can feel security oozing out of their pores. They know that being the loudest person in the room doesn't make them the smartest or the most talented.

Confidence can feel like fixing your hair and make-up to your satisfaction and taking a moment to look in the mirror and appreciate your own beauty. As you come into contact with people throughout the day, you are pleased to share your beauty with them. This beauty empowers you to walk tall with your shoulders back. This beauty empowers you to smile because you know that you look good! When you look good, you feel good and you are motivated to share your beauty with those around you. You are open to and energized by people desiring to be in your presence and your presence sparks joy.

When you think of yourself, is there someone or something you have great confidence in? In the space below, write down that someone or something.

Reflection Questions

1. Who do you have confidence (trust) in? Name the person and explain what makes you trust them.

Understanding Confidence

2. How much confidence do you have in this person?

3. Do you have confidence (trust) in your Self?

                Yes   No

4. How much confidence (trust) do you have in your Self?

5. Explain what makes you trust your Self OR what stops you from trusting your Self?

6. Do you have confidence (trust) in God?

                Yes   No

7. How much confidence (trust) do you have in God?

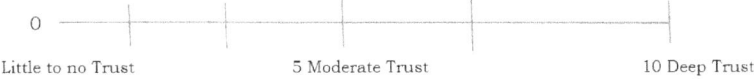

8. Explain what makes you trust God OR what stops you from trusting Him?

I could go on and on defining confidence, but the bottom line is that at the core, confidence is really about your ability to trust: trust your Self, trust others, and trust God. Let's get into it.

Trusting God

If there is anyone deserving of our trust, it's God. God is the creator of the universe. He is a God who created something out of absolutely nothing. He set the stars, moon, and sun in the sky. He separated day from night (Gen. 1:31) He knows all, sees all, and is above all. He is the bright and morning star (Rev. 22:16), the lily of the valley (Song of Sol. 2:1), the lover of our souls (Song of Sol 6:3).

He loved you so much that while we were yet sinners, He sent His one and only son to die for us (Rom. 5:8). He gave us Jesus and Jesus left us with the Holy Spirit. And because of all this, we have power over the enemy. Need I say more?

Jesus is insanely, intensely, and madly in love with you! Ephesians 3:18-19 says, "And may you have the power to understand, as all God's people should, how wide, how long, how high, and how deep His love is. May you experience the love of Christ, though it is too great to understand fully. Then you will be made complete with all the fullness of life and power that comes from God." (Eph. 3:18-19)

If you believe the truth of God's word, the only heart response is, "Lord, I love you, too!"

Understanding Confidence

"Jesus, I trust you!"

"Lord, my confidence is in you!"

Many of us have barriers to trusting God, which make it difficult to *receive* His love for us. If we struggle to receive love from the one who created us, we'll struggle to offer and receive love to our Self and others. If this applies to you, please check out "God's Love for Me" in the appendix.

The most amazing thing about trusting Jesus is that you can trust in Him even when you can't trust yourself. Have you ever had a longing so deep, a passion so strong that you knew it did not align with God's plan for you? I certainly have. In those seasons I felt like I was in the middle of an emotional, mental, spiritual, and physical war zone. My thoughts were racing out of control. I had an inability to distinguish a truth from a lie. The lines were blurred and I was desperate to have things my way.

In those moments it was hard to believe that God's plan for me was good and would bring me hope and a good future (Jer. 29:11). I didn't feel like I could trust him with my joy and contentment.

Every now and then, I find myself wanting to take matters into my own hands and do things my way. His word is the only thing that keeps me from falling, because at times I have little to offer myself. In these times, the truth of His holy word undergirds me and props me up when I cannot stand. The sweet whispers from the Holy Spirit sooth my soul, release the pain, and help me surrender my will to the Father.

You may not trust yourself at all times, but you can *always* trust in God! One of my favorite promises comes from 1 Peter 2:6, "*Those who put their trust in the Lord will not be disappointed.*" (1 Pet. 2:6) This truth gives me confidence in knowing that my choice to follow God and do things His way will never leave me in shame.

There is so much peace and safety available to us through our relationship with God.

If you are a follower of Jesus, you need to learn how to trust him more and more with each passing day. Learning to trust your father and creator will unlock the door to knowing and trusting yourself. As we learn the charter and nature of the Father, we discover more about who we are and who He has created us to be. We are made in His image and likeness so it's only right that the more we know Him, the more we know ourselves. He made you and He loves you more than anyone else ever can or ever will. Trust His love for you.

Trusting Yourself

Trusting yourself means being able to attempt to do all kinds of things without judging yourself too harshly ("Trusting Yourself" Healthline, https://www.healthline.com/health/trusting-yourself.).

Trusting my abilities and qualities came fairly easy for me but trusting my ideas, that's another story. I am well aware of my abilities to communicate well in verbal and written form, solve problems, resolve conflict, lead people, and teach. These are all things I started to recognize about myself before middle school, so I've had a lot of practice trusting myself in those ways. In terms of qualities, I am warm, energized, intelligent, optimistic, and a driven challenger. Even though I consider myself to be a smart and creative person, I sometimes struggle with trusting my ideas, and let me tell you, I have LOTS of them! One of the things I enjoy most is thinking and creating strategies.

One thing I've noticed is the way I see and think about things can be vastly different from other people. At times, I found myself doubting my ideas with thoughts like,

"Is this rational? No one else sees it this way."
"Am I way off-base? Maybe this idea is outlandish."
"Just settle down. This just isn't the right time."
"Everyone else says it has to happen this way. What makes you think that your ideas will work?"
"This has never been done before. Why now?"
"What happens if you fail? What will people say?"
"If you mess up, you will really look stupid."

Over the years, I have discovered that these voices in my head are just fear talking. As I learned how to press beyond fear and give myself permission to take risks, my confidence in my creative thinking increased. I grew in my ability to *trust* my ideas. Gaining confidence (trust) in this one area took me from being an underpaid, overworked state employee of 17 years to an owner and CEO of three highly profitable and impactful corporations.

God has given you abilities, qualities, and ideas to help you fulfill your purpose on Earth and live an abundant life. *Don't allow an inability to trust yourself rob you of your identity and destiny.*

Trusting Others

God designed the Christian life to be lived within the context of community. Jesus started his ministry on earth around age 30 and one of the first things he did was select people to go with him (Luke 6:12-16). We know these people as the disciples and Jesus surrounded himself with others for fellowship, connection, strength, teaching, and training. He knew that His assignment on Earth would end, so He wanted to invest in others who could continue the work after He left (John 14:10).

"Trust can help bring us closer to other people. Trusting others, such as family members and friends, can reassure us that we'll be helped when we need it. It's the foundation of any healthy relationship — including the relationship you have with yourself. ("Trusting Yourself." Healthline, https://www.healthline.com/health/trusting-yourself.)"

In the same way, we need others in this journey of life. *You don't need to trust everyone, but if you don't trust anyone, you are in a danger zone.* People who have difficulty trusting others typically suffer with isolation, anxiety, paranoia, loneliness, depression, and discontentment. You need to learn how to trust the *right* people so that you can have a quality social life, feel a sense of belonging, and allow the love and care that others have for you to bless your life.

Please hear me out. If you have intense difficulty trusting people, it is most likely because you have been *deeply* hurt and mishandled by a friend, lover, sibling, colleague, church member, pastor, or maybe a mother or father. No matter who hurt us and how deep the betrayal, we must not allow the actions of others to control us and interfere with the good life God has planned. We will never experience that goodness without receiving healing that will free us to trust and be close with healthy people. Get help now to reclaim your life.

Once again, you don't need to trust *all* people. We need to learn to trust the ones who bring love and light, treat you with respect, and are connected to God's plan for your life. We also don't need to have the same level of trust in each relationship. Each person and relationship is different and therefore it is appropriate for trust and intimacy to look different from one relationship to the next.

In Dr. Dharius Daniels book Relational Intelligence, he defines four different types of relationships to include friends, associates, assignments, and advisors. Dr. Daniels argues that if we tend to misuse anything that we do not define. Therefore, defining our relationships is a major key to discerning who we can and cannot trust.

The five characteristics of people we can trust include unshakeable charter, unmovable reliability; unbridled honesty; unconditional love; and unceasing encouragement. Without this type of relational intelligence, we can repeat toxic relational cycles and experience unnecessary hardship along the way.

Yes, it is okay to differentiate your relationships. While all people are valuable in the eyes of God, they don't add the same value to your life. (Daniels 2020) In addition, the value that someone adds to your life in one season, may not transfer into your next season. Let me give an example.

I have a very dear friend who is not a Christian. He is an older professional who is a kind, intelligent, wise and excellent listener. This friend knows me very well and has permission to call me out on foolishness. Yes, I have my moments! I would occasionally talk to him when I was struggling to make a clinical decision or had conflict with a patient. After working with him daily for a year, I grew to trust his judgment and welcomed his thoughts and advice regarding some areas of my personal life and it was very helpful. Over the last few years, I have called him a lot less because I have some new people who also provide me with feedback, especially in my professional work with couples. I don't call him less because I stopped trusting his judgment. I call him less because my needs have changed, and God has supplied me with a new mentor who has the experience and insight to respond to these new needs. Intimacy and trust can look different from one relationship to the next and evolve over time. But you have to understand who you are and where you are enough to realign that relationship with your current reality. That type of navigation requires relational intelligence, self awareness, and confidence (trust) in God and your Self.

Improving your confidence is an essential key to the development of the Healthy Self. While confidence building is a great starting place, it is not meant to be a stand-alone solution. The major ticket to our personal, spiritual, and emotional growth happens in an area even closer to our inner lives; our self-esteem. Intrigued much? Turn the page.

CHAPTER 2

Defining Healthy Self-Esteem

self – esteem.
self – love.
self – care.
self – appreciation.

These phrases appear on the cover of every magazine, social media image, and best–selling book these days. At a simple glance, you may draw the conclusion that all of this "Self" talk is what has American culture inundated with selfish, self-righteous, and self–indulgent people who strive to have their own way by any means necessary. While that may seem like a logical conclusion, the concept of the Self has a lot more nuance.

While much of the behavior we see in American culture *appears* to be very *self*-motivated, I see that as an illusion. Most of us are not driven by their *true or authentic* Self. We are driven by our role self, ego and/or the false Self. Our true Self is who we are when we are healthy. This person reflects the goodness and image of God through attributes like love, compassion, patience, gentleness, self-control, faith, and all other fruits of the spirit (Gal. 5:22-23). The true Self is a bright light deposited by God within us that radiates into the world. The false Self is the unhealthy part of us that causes us to lean away from our God design and toward self-protection and self-promotion through attitudes like selfishness, pride, anger, fear, and all other works of the flesh (Gal. 5:19-21). The false Self not only causes us to lean away from God, it causes us to lean away from our Self. We become less capable of knowing how we feel so we can express it in healthy ways and make choices that keep us aligned. In my opinion, most Americans are not driven by who we really are; we are driven by who we *think* we are.

Why is this so? In our culture, this behavior is a byproduct of our emphasis on performance. The American way of living, doing, and being says this:

"What brings you value is what you do."

"You are what you do."

"You are worthy and deserving only if you accomplish things."

In my clinical work, most of my time is spent helping people come out of this work and performance-based mentality. This way of thinking ignores the true Self and is an assault to our personhood. I find these beliefs to be in direct contradiction with what God says about who we are, our worth, and our value. Don't get me wrong, God has called us to work and steward well. He rewards those things. However, there is no biblical evidence to support that the core of our identity, worth, and value is established through our work and performance. Actually, when work shows up on the scene in Genesis, it is given to Adam as a *curse*, not a blessing or reward (Gen. 3:19).

I wish that this work and performance-based mindset was just a secular concept. Unfortunately, this over-emphasis on work is prevalent in the church. The only difference is that some of the messaging in the church is often more covert. In one breath, we are taught that we are valuable and created in the image of an incredible God. We are his workmanship, His treasure, the apple of His eye, and His love for us is enough. In the next breath, we bash, humiliate, and disconnect ourselves from fellow Christians who have a different theological bent than us. We idolize pastors with mega churches, then blame and shame them for burning out. We count members and money as a primary way of measuring church growth. There is something very wrong and broken about this mindset in our churches. However, I am encouraged. If we are the body of Christ, the church can realign with God's truth concerning our true identity, and we can impact the world with a church culture that is much better equipped to help people heal and grow. This teaching on healthy self-esteem will empower us as we seek a better path.

Defining Self-Esteem

Self-esteem is your overall opinion of yourself. It is your subjective sense of worth or value. (*What Is Self-Esteem?*, Cherry 2022)

It is a mindset, not a feeling. A mindset is a fixed state of mind that does not waver. Self-esteem is a fixed opinion about yourself, your worth, and your value that does not waver.

Whether we realize it or not, our opinion of ourselves and ability to see our own value (self-esteem) is a dictator in our lives. A dictator is a ruler with total power and typically, that power has been obtained by force. (Collins English Dictionary, 2010) The way we see, think, and feel about ourselves controls our *entire* life! Our self-esteem is a filter for our relationship with ourselves and others. Self-esteem is a filter through which we make sense of who we are, what we are capable of and what we deserve. Self-esteem is a dictating mindset. **Self-esteem must be established.**

Confidence is a feeling. Feelings can be defined as unreasoned opinions or beliefs. They are an emotional state or a reaction to a trigger. Your feelings of confidence can come and go. In the words of Peter Scazaro in his book Emotionally Healthy Spirituality, "Feelings are also *indicators* not dictators." (Scazzero 2006) Indicators help you gauge where you are and track yourself in a situation. Often, your feelings will change from one situation to the next, and sometimes from one moment to the next. Feelings help us navigate life, but they are not stable. **Feelings must be managed.**

So, if feelings must be managed, we must increase our ability to know how we feel, manage our emotions, and find healthy ways to release them. Feelings, traumas, and cultural context are *indicators*, not *dictators*. Indicators are places from which we gather information, not a place from which we make decisions.

If self-esteem must be established, we need to make sure that our opinion of ourselves, our personal worth, and our value align with the truth of God's word and not what our feelings, brokenness, traumas, experiences, or cultural context *indicates* to us.

Is This Selfish?

I find so many people, especially Christians, highly resistant to do any inner work that involves a major focus on the Self. We've embraced false narratives like:

"*Focusing on myself is selfish.*"

"*God just wants me to love others well.*"

"*Building my self-esteem seems prideful and pride is a sin.*"

"*If I just focus on Jesus and the kingdom, everything will work out just fine.*"

It was difficult to write out the sentences above because they make me angry. Angry with the church for feeding us lies. Angry with myself for believing these lies at some point. Angry with the devil for trying to suppress God's people. Let's uncover the lie.

The Truth About Self-focus

1. *Good stewards embrace self-focus.*

You can't be a good steward without some healthy self-focus. God has created you to steward the land and animals (Gen. 1:25-26), children (Prov. 22:6), money (Prov. 13:22), and yourself (Matt. 25:14-30). God is not the only person responsible for you. You are responsible for you. If you don't see yourself as valuable and worthy, the chances of you offering yourself the best care is slim. You are responsible for managing your emotions, controlling your thoughts, showing up as your true self, making good choices, discerning things, and behaving in ways that honor God, self, and others. God is with you and the Holy Spirit is your helper, and *you* are responsible for ensuring that you are healthy, strong, and focused on the things God wants you to focus on. If you don't allow yourself to have healthy focus on yourself, how will you steward yourself? You won't. You will be unsteady and unstable, like a leaf blowing in the wind. Unsteady and unstable people don't make good stewards.

2. *You can only love others as well as you love yourself.*

People who love themselves have the greatest capacity to love others. Love is a serious matter. Everything that Christ has done for us and the good things that are to come are all born out of His love for us. When He calls us to love, he means it. Jesus didn't just call us to love others, he commanded us to love ourselves.

> ³⁷ Jesus replied, "'You must love the Lord your God with all your heart, all your soul, and all your mind.'[e] ³⁸ This is the first and greatest commandment. ³⁹ A second is equally important: 'Love your neighbor as yourself.'[f] ⁴⁰ The entire law and all the demands of the prophets are based on these two commandments." (Matt. 22:37-40)

Essentially, Jesus is saying that the first two commandments are essential to walking in obedience as His followers. The very foundation is built upon loving Him with all that we are and loving ourselves well so that we can love others well, too. The second commandment is a call to love others *out of* a place of love for ourselves. What Jesus is saying here is that in order to love others well, you have to first love yourself.

Have you ever noticed that? Jesus *commands* you to love yourself. Why do you think He would do that? I believe that Jesus commands self-love because He knows the heart and minds of mankind. So many of His followers have fallen into the trap of trying to prove their worth and value by being productive like Martha (Luke 10:38-42) or getting everything right. But Jesus never intended for our sense of worth or value to come from any of those things. He designed it to penetrate from the inside out, from His hand to our hearts and into the lives of others.

Let's take a moment to define self-love. According to an article published by Psychology Today, "For some people, self-love means taking a warm bath or pampering themselves with a massage or manicure. Yet, the elusive self-love that we seek requires something deeper than anything we can "do" for ourselves. Self-love means finding peace within ourselves, and resting comfortably within the depths of our being. We might find temporary respite by doing something to nurture ourselves but a deeper inner peace requires cultivating a certain way of being with ourselves, and a warm and nurturing attitude toward what we experience inside. In essence, self-love is simply a way of being non-judgmentally kind, present, and mindful toward whatever we happen to be experiencing. (Amodeo 2015)

How might your life be different if you were able to be with yourself in a non-judgmentally, kind, present, and mindful way no matter what you happened to be experiencing? I am not talking about living in denial about the bad or ugly things that are taking place inside of you or around you, but maintaining a kind, loving, and non-judgmental stance toward your Self no matter what. Take a moment to write a response in the question in the space below.

How might your life be different if you were able to be with yourself in a non-judgmentally, kind, present, and mindful way no matter what you happened to be experiencing?

3. *People who attend to themselves are more likely to fulfill their calling and destiny.*

As God's people, we have a significant advantage. No matter how much doom, gloom, and chaos we see in the world, we already know how the story ends, Jesus is victorious over *all* things! Because He wins, we win, too. God promises to make all things work together for our good and His glory (Rom. 8:28). When it comes to ability to fulfill calling, God's sovereignty and plan is not an issue. God is faithful to do what He promised in the Earth. If you want His promises to be fulfilled in your life, you must learn how to steward your Self and attend to your Self, not just others.

Some of us spend so much time helping, fixing, serving, doing, and giving to others and have little or nothing to offer ourselves. Don't get me wrong, there is nothing wrong with being a servant or helper, but God teaches us to do all things in moderation (Phil. 4:5). Yes, there is a time for serving, giving, and helping and we must be able to discern the season, time, and purpose over all things (Eccles. 3:1) A call to moderation is a call to end over-indulgence. While some people overindulge in alcohol, sex, spending, or food; others over-indulge in helping, giving, and serving. Too much of anything can turn something good and Godly into something sinful and unhealthy.

We have to create space to attend to ourselves to make sure we are not over-functioning for others and under-functioning in our own lives. Don't be like the man with 10 talents. He lost out on some blessings because he was not willing to attend to what God had placed in him (Matt. 25:14-30). He thought he was doing a good thing but ended up being rebuked for not stewarding his gifts and attending to himself. Help us, Lord!

4. *Healthy people transfer healing. Healthy people are healed people. Healed people heal people.*

> Walking in any form of health requires focus on the self.
> To have healthy emotions, we attend to our feelings
> To have healthy spirits, we practice spiritual disciplines.
> To have healthy minds, we learn and manage our thoughts.
> To have healthy bodies, we eat, sleep and exercise well.
> There is no one size fits all formula to healthy living but living a healthy lifestyle *positions* us for healing. Discovering what works

best for us individually is a life-long journey and process. It's not always easy, but the beauty is that we learn so much along the way. The journey and process is a place for learning about yourself. In pursuit of health in any area of our lives, we will encounter pain or discomfort and ultimately receive healing. Some of us are stuck and stunted because we refuse to take a journey that leads toward health. Remember, healing is not just limited to the physical body, it includes our minds, spirits, emotions, and more.

Walking three miles a day can heal high blood pressure. Allowing yourself to cry when you are sad releases a chemical called endorphins. These feel-good chemicals can help ease both physical and emotional pain and decrease symptoms related to anxiety and depression. Learning new information and skills builds knowledge and understanding. When knowledge and understanding enter your mind, you can overcome the bondage of ignorance which leads to poor decision making and pain. Prayer encourages your spirit, allows hope to arise, and helps you feel closer to God. There is so much evidence for the many ways that living a healthy lifestyle positions us for healing. When you experience healing in your life, you are positioned to transfer that healing to others. No health = no healing. In other words, if you don't live a healthy lifestyle and receive healing, your ability to positively impact the lives of others is minimized.

Would you like to see God use you to release healing into the lives of others? He can and He will! Get healthy so you can get healed! Just like hurt people hurt people, healed people heal people.

I desperately want you to take this journey and stay the course with me. I am so deeply passionate about helping people develop healthy self-esteem because God did a work for me. He removed the chains from my mind about myself, my worth, and my identity. My beliefs were a script that had me locked in an invisible prison of self-doubt, sadness, and fear. I didn't have anyone to walk me through the process of healing. It was just me and Jesus. It took me almost falling off of the deep end and turning away from God to find myself at a place of surrender to the Father.

During this time, I wasn't backslidden or balled up in a corner, I was leading and serving God's people. I was hurting and broken in ways I didn't know and couldn't see because I was not attending to myself. I was doing every good work for everyone else while ignoring myself and slowly dying on the inside. God helped me highlight the lies I believed about myself. He gave me a new way of thinking, believing, and seeing myself, my situation, and other people.

In the body, self-esteem is shaped by your thoughts, relationships, and experiences. In the spirit, our self-esteem is shaped by how God sees us, how He loves us, and His plans for our lives. God gave me a supernatural filter. Through this process, I believe He will do the same for you. God has given me healthy self-esteem as a stronghold. A stronghold is a place that has been fortified so as to protect against attack; a place where a particular belief is strongly defended or upheld. A stronghold is high and inaccessible to our enemies. (Hartikainen 2023)

God showed me how he felt about me, saw me, and hoped for me. He helped me bring my mind and heart into agreement with His. I call that Healthy Self Esteem. Healthy Self Esteem is my stronghold.

This process started for me in 2016 and continues daily because I am a disciple of Jesus. I won't stop learning from Him and following Him until I see Him face to face. Then, I will be like Him (1 John 3:2). As God heals, restores, and recovers my life, my promise to Him is that I will spend my life allowing the healing He's deposited in me to flow through me and into the lives of others. Healing is contagious!

    I will never forget how alone I felt. I had no one to talk to or turn but God. My goal is to make sure that people everywhere know how to reach Jesus and healthy people when they are hurting and need help. In the remainder of this book, I will teach you how to make Jesus' thoughts and feelings about you your own. I will show you how to partner with Jesus to build healthy self-esteem and make that your stronghold. In your overall opinion of yourself, you will align with the heart of the Father concerning you. Your beliefs around your worth and value will become fortified, stable, and firm. You will see yourself in your struggles and maintain your commitment to love yourself anyway. You will grow to appreciate and like yourself, regardless of your circumstances.

Jesus, build a stronghold.

The remaining chapters will guide us through the work of building healthy self-esteem. We will continue to combine theological truth and psychological understanding to create practical pathways to healing and freedom.

    Before we move on, we need to take some time to reflect.

    If you take the reflection activity seriously, it will take you about 45-60 minutes at a minimum. If you don't have that much time and/or are not in a private setting, pull out your phone and schedule a time to come back to come back to this within the next 7 days. I mean it–come back to this. Reflection is how we go about applying what we are learning. New information does not transform us–it's the application of what we learned that changes our lives. In a growth, change or learning process, application is what stewardship looks like. Take yourself and your future seriously enough to come back to this if you cannot complete it immediately.

Reflection Questions

Scripture makes it clear, the second commandment is a call to love others out of a place of love for ourselves. What Jesus is saying here is that in order to love others well, *you have to first love yourself* (Matt. 23:39).

1. How much do you love others?

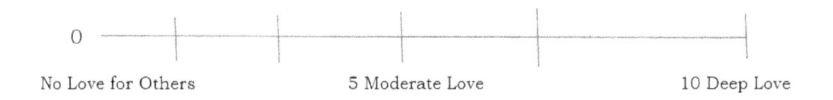

```
0 ├──────┼──────┼──────┼──────┤
No Love for Others      5 Moderate Love      10 Deep Love
```

2. When it comes to loving others, I rated myself as a _____, on the scale above.

3. What does this say about me and my life right now?

4. How much do you love yourself?

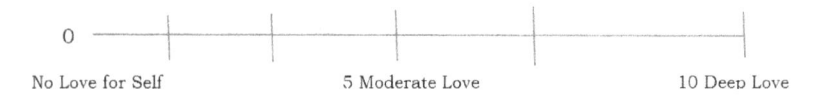

```
0 ├──────┼──────┼──────┼──────┤
No Love for Self        5 Moderate Love      10 Deep Love
```

5. When it comes to loving myself, I rate myself at a _____, because.....

6. What does this say about who I am and where I am right now?

For many, loving someone else feels much easier than loving themselves. Once again, we will *not* allow our feelings to dictate our lives. If loving yourself feels hard at times, that's simply an indicator that you need to work on aligning the way you see yourself with the way God sees you. You may need to lean into learning how to offer your Self a deeper level of kindness, gentleness, and a commitment to be present with your Self and for your Self without judgment.

7. What would loving yourself more look like?

8. What would loving others more look like?

Self-esteem is your overall opinion of yourself. It is your subjective sense of worth or value.

9. What is your overall opinion of yourself?

10. How worthy do you feel?

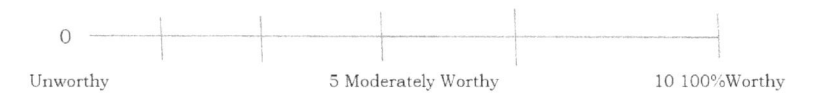

```
0 ————|————|————|————|————|————
Unworthy        5 Moderately Worthy        10 100%Worthy
```

11. When it comes to feeling worthy/valuable, I rate myself as a _____ because…..

12. Make a list of experiences, personal qualities, or beliefs that contribute to your feelings of worthiness/value.

13. Take a moment to write out a prayer of thanksgiving to God for the things you listed above.

14. Make a list of experiences, personal qualities, or beliefs that contribute to any feeling of unworthiness.

15. Take a moment to write a prayer of intercession and confession to God for the thing you listed above. Honestly and wholeheartedly share your feelings of unworthiness with God for at least 3-5 minutes. Do whatever you need to do; cry, scream, shout, bang something, just get it out!

16. Once you are finished, sit quietly and wait for Him to respond to your cry or feeling of pain, shame, guilt, etc. Psalm 34:17, *"The LORD hears his people when they call to him for help. He rescues them from all their troubles.When we cry out to God"*. Write His response below.

CHAPTER 3

Valuing Yourself

The first component of healthy self-esteem is valuing yourself. People who value themselves appreciate, cherish, love, and prize themselves as a treasure created in the image of God. Whenever I talk to people about valuing themselves, folks get nervous. I wonder if some of us believe that valuing ourselves is equivalent to living a self-absorbed life where we feel so good about who we are that we say "no" to anything or anyone that does not align with what we want in life. Maybe we are envisioning a decked-out diva or a manicured man sitting on a pedestal being fanned by feathers and fed exotic grapes by servants. When you encounter people who have a self-absorbed disposition, be careful not to assume that self-focus is a byproduct of valuing oneself. Inordinate levels of self-focus can often be a symptom of low self-esteem. I'll say more about that later.

Accepting your value makes you wise and obedient because you are making the choice to align your thoughts and feelings about yourself with the Father's thoughts and feelings about you. People who value themselves are more likely to do things like:

-Continue their education
-Be honest with themselves
-Be honest with others

-Invest in their future
-Take the time to care for their bodies
-Set limits and boundaries
-Forgive themselves for making mistakes
-Forgive others so they can be free
-Let go of a dead-end job
-Confront issues in toxic relationships
-Work through their own emotional issues
-Ask for help
-Give themselves permission to let go
-Say no
-Say yes
-Pursue their dreams

What on this list have you been needing or wanting to do? This is a great time to continue reading and be curious about yourself without judgment. Increasing your ability to value yourself may provide a pathway forward. I am overwhelmed by how God uncovered something in this area of my life just a few short years ago. I thought that I did a great job valuing myself. After all, I felt really good about myself as a person and treated myself with a lot of respect, or so I thought.

I had a season of life where I found myself being overwhelmed with feelings of anger and frustration. The anger showed up as aggression toward others. During this season of life, I was so stressed out. I was working full-time, serving in ministry, starting a new business, and caring for my family and home. I felt the pressure of wanting my business to grow quickly, trying to meet all the needs of people in our ministry, attempting to keep a clean and orderly home, and being emotionally available for my husband and children. It was a very heavy load to carry. At one point, I noticed I was angry and frustrated with most of the people around me; colleagues at work, employees at my company, people at church, and even the family in my home. I was boiling with frustration and anxiety. How did I respond to this pressure? Not so well. Eventually, the long-term impact of stress caused me to act out of character and over the course of two weeks, I found myself cussing out a family member; hanging up on my boss, and yelling at the pastor's wife.

I finally got to the place where I acknowledged that the only way out of this negative headspace was to slow down and spend time with Jesus. Let His words and the presence of the Holy Spirit speak a word to me and encourage my heart. As I sat before the Lord, crying out for help. The Holy Spirit showed me that my aggression was being driven by a fear of failure. If I failed, I would be ashamed of myself. He allowed me to hear the little voice in the back of my head and heart screaming, "You better not mess this up! You better not make us look bad!"

In that moment, I realized my anger was being masked by a fear of failure and a sense of shame for the possibility of not being able to make everything work. This deeply hidden shame was actually causing me to devalue myself. I devalued myself by not taking care of my body, over committing myself to others, and ignoring my limitations. I was completely exhausted and beyond my capacity and would not offer myself any relief or ask for help. As I look back, that was such an act of dishonor and disrespect to my Self. I secretly believed that my ability to make all the things work and grow is what made me worthy. I believed that holding everything together was what gave me value; but that wasn't true.

Whether I fail or succeed, my value is secure. This allows me to relax and not press so hard to make everything just right. My worth is no longer on the line. My worth is not negotiable.

Five Biblical Truths About Your Value

Newsflash, you are created in the very image of God the Father (Gen. 1:27). He is the author of creation, the one who is holy, perfect, right, just, and kind. He is all knowing, all seeing, all loving, and ever-present. You carry the DNA of God inside of you.

That's not just true for you, it's true for everyone despite what they believe about God or His existence. Even people who don't acknowledge or reject God are created in His image and carry His DNA. He is the creator of *all* things. The creator doesn't need anyone's approval to create you with high worth and value.

The truth is that you have intrinsic worth and value that was deposited in you before the foundations of the earth. When something is intrinsic, it means that it belongs to the essential nature or constitution of a thing. Your value is an essential part of you, it is a natural part of who you are. Just like your heart, lungs, and brain, your value is a part of and included in your original design. When it comes to your value, here are some practical and biblical truths to consider.

1. **Your value and worth were established before the foundations of the Earth.**

   > *"Then God said, 'Let us make mankind in our image, in our likeness, so that they may rule over the fish in the sea and the birds in the sky, over the livestock and all the wild animals,[a] and over all the creatures that move along the ground. So God created mankind in his own image, in the image of God he created them; male and female he created them.'"* (Gen. 1:26-27)

> "Even before he made the world, God loved us and chose us in Christ to be holy and without fault in his eyes." (Eph. 1:4)

> "Before you were born I set you apart and appointed you as my prophet to the nations." (Jer. 1:5)

2. **Your value and worth is not dictated by your family of origin. While your mother gave birth to you and your father raised you, they did not create you. Your creator established your value.**

> "For you formed my inward parts; you knitted me together in my mother's womb. I praise you, for I am fearfully and wonderfully made. Wonderful are your works; my soul knows it very well. My frame was not hidden from you, when I was being made in secret, intricately woven in the depths of the earth. Your eyes saw my unformed substance; in your book were written, every one of them, the days that were formed for me, when as yet there was none of them." (Ps. 139:13-16)

> "For we are God's workmanship, created in Christ Jesus to do good works, which God prepared in advance as our way of life." (Eph. 2:10)

> "But to all who did receive him, who believed in his name, he gave the right to become children of God." (John 1:12)

3. **Making mistakes, messing up, or getting things wrong does not decrease your value.**

> "If we confess our sins, he is faithful and just to forgive us our sins and to cleanse us from all unrighteousness." (1 John 1:9)

> "You are altogether beautiful, my love; there is no flaw in you." (Song of Sol. 4:7)

> "Can anything ever separate us from Christ's love? Does it mean he no longer loves us if we have trouble or calamity, or are persecuted, or hungry, or destitute, or in danger, or threatened with death? (As the Scriptures say, "For your sake we are killed every day; we are being slaughtered like sheep."[a]) No, despite all these things, overwhelming victory is ours through Christ, who loved us. And I am convinced that nothing can ever separate us from God's love. Neither death nor life, neither angels nor demons,[b] neither our fears for today nor our worries about tomorrow—not even the powers of hell can separate us from God's love. No power in the sky above or in the earth below—indeed, nothing in all creation will ever be able to separate us from the love of God that is revealed in Christ Jesus our Lord." (Rom. 8:35-39)

4 **Being rejected by others does not decrease your value.**

> "Even if my father and mother abandon me, the Lord will hold me close." (Ps. 27:10)

> "The stone that the builders rejected has now become the cornerstone." (Ps. 118:22)

5. **Everything that Jesus did for us on the cross proves how valuable you truly are to him.**

   > "But God shows his love for us in that while we were still sinners, Christ died for us" (Rom. 5:8)

   > "For God so loved the world, that he gave his only Son, that whoever believes in him should not perish but have eternal life." (John 3:16)

You didn't do anything to earn your value. You can't do anything to increase your value. You can't do anything to diminish your value. Your value is God given, stable, firm, and unwavering. There is not nor will there ever be an issue with your value or worth. The issue is whether or not you will accept your value. Will you accept your God-given value despite what has happened to you? Will you accept your intrinsic worth when others put you down? Can you keep your heart and mind aligned with biblical truth when you've made a mistake or misstep? These are critical questions.

Valuing yourself is simply being able to accept yourself as the gift that God made you. Because there are so many misconceptions and outright lies about self-value, it is just as important for us to talk about what accepting your value does ***not do.***

Accepting your value *does not* decrease the value of others. Just like no one and nothing can decrease your value, you cannot decrease the value of other people. You are not God. Another person's value is not in the palm of your hand. But make no mistake, your choice to value yourself does *impact* others. Some people will see you making choices from a place of self-value and feel deeply encouraged or inspired. You will be surprised how many people have not had self-value modeled for them. It is more common for someone to see others model hard work, determination, creativity, or confidence. While these are positive behaviors, self-value is not a prerequisite for any of them. On the contrary, some people will see you making choices from a place of self-value, and it makes them feel inadequate, angry, or confused. Some people may be triggered by your display of self-value. When this happens, notice it and keep valuing yourself. Someone being triggered by the truth of God's word is not a place from which you should be making decisions from. Stay committed to what God says about you and pray for that person. Ask God to help them receive a revelation of how much they are loved and valued by Him, too. But whatever you do, please do not start dumbing or watering yourself down to make someone else feel better. I know a lot of people do this because they think they are helping someone. Trust me, pretending to be someone other than who God has made you to be is dishonoring to yourself, others, and God. Showing up as your authentic, self-valuing, and self-loving self, confronts the spirit of low self-esteem, self-loathing, and depression that the enemy uses to keep so many Christians in bondage. Being your authentic self is what contributes to the liberation of God's people for His purposes in the earth.

Accepting your value *does not* make you selfish or self-absorbed. Making the choice to value yourself is about aligning your thoughts with the thoughts of the Father which are the truth of His word. These thoughts are excellent, pure, lovely, a good report, praiseworthy, and true, the types of thoughts to ward off anxiety and fear. These thoughts lead to experiencing the peace of God (Phil. 4:6-9). Right beliefs lead to right behavior. If you are healthy and valuing yourself it will lead to positive outcomes in your life and your relationships. If you do not value yourself or are unhealthy, you may be prone to inappropriate levels of self-focus. Remember, no one is perfect. Even healthy people may wrestle with selfishness from time to time. That's simply human nature. Whatever comes into our awareness becomes more accessible to the Holy Spirit's work in our hearts and minds.

Accepting your value *does not* make you arrogant or haughty. This is a common lie that tricks people out of valuing themselves. Who wants to be arrogant or haughty? Once again, you have to remember that accepting your value is about aligning with God's truth about your worth. Please know, your choice to love and accept yourself can cause people who don't love or value themselves to manifest. Why? Because it makes them more aware of their own lack of self-love, acceptance, and value. Mentally, if they give you permission to show up for yourself and be happy for you, by default they will acknowledge that there is something broken inside of them. Not everyone is always in a place where they are able to see certain parts of themselves clearly. Your choice to accept your value will challenge people to accept their own. If a person lacks self-awareness in this area, your very presence may feel like an assault or an attack. Why?

People who do not accept their value are not very safe with themselves. If someone is not safe with themself, they may not feel safe with you. In these cases, it's not unusual for a person to misunderstand your actions and motives as a form of self-protection and self-preservation. If you are confused or taken aback by accusations about being arrogant or prideful, take that to the Lord in prayer and discuss it with trusted mentors, coaches, or counselors. Be careful not to take everyone's opinion of you at face value. Oftentimes, people's opinions of you (good or bad) are more about their *perception* and less about who you really are. Ask the

Lord to help you see things for what they truly are so that you can stay rooted and grounded in His truth about you and continue to grow in grace.

Reflection Questions

1. In your own words, what does it mean to value yourself?

2. Rate your level of value for self on the scale below

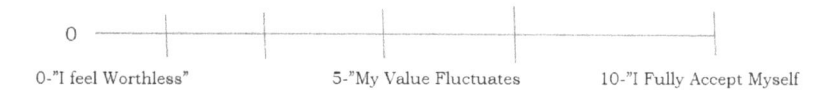

   0 —|—————|—————|—————|—————|
   0-"I feel Worthless"   5-"My Value Fluctuates"   10-"I Fully Accept Myself"

3. I rate my value of self as a _____ because….. _____.

4. When I reflect on my level of value for myself I feel… _____

5. Pray a prayer of petition to God. Ask Him to open your heart and mind to you and about you as you continue to read.

The Trick of Devalue

If God's word is so rich, true, and powerful, and we are made in his image, why do so many of us struggle to see our own value?

Devaluing the Self is a trick of the enemy of our souls. He wants you to believe the lie that you are worthless, nothing, insignificant, and unimportant. Why? If he can distort the image you have of yourself, he can *stop* you from being who you really are. If he stops you from being your true self; whole, confident, healthy, and free, God has one less participant in His plan to bring heaven to Earth; a plan to overthrow the kingdom of darkness with the Kingdom of light.

Today, right here and now, we will uncover Satan and his lies once and for all. I declare now that as you read these words, your mind, heart, and soul will be set free. The blinders will be removed from your natural and spiritual eyes. You will be empowered to see yourself for who you really are and move forward with a new level of love, clarity, and confidence. We claim that now in Jesus' name!

Tricks the Enemy Uses To Devalue Us

Putting Ourselves Down.

Whenever we think poorly about ourselves or talk to ourselves with disrespect, we put ourselves down. Some of us don't say these things aloud but we are constantly trash talking ourselves in our heads by saying things like:

"You look so fat".
"God, your stomach looks gross."
"Who would want you?"
"You are so stupid."
"I hate you."
"No one wants you around."
"Shut up, you'll sound stupid."
"You're such a screw up."

How on earth can we value ourselves if we are talking to ourselves like trash? We can't. If you have a habit of putting yourself down, it needs to stop now. This is one of the worst forms of self-harm there is. You may never let others hear you say these things to yourself, but **you** hear yourself. **You** are hurting yourself. The bible teaches us not to allow blessings and curses to come out of the same mouth (James 3:10). Before words ever come out of your mouth, they are alive in your head, your heart, and your spirit. When you talk down to yourself, you curse yourself. You can't always control whether or not others put you down, but you can control yourself.

Reflection Questions

1. Do you ever find yourself talking down to yourself aloud or just in your head?

2. What do you say in your head?

3. What do you say aloud? This can include negative things you say about yourself to other people–even if you are "just playing".

4. Would you speak this way to a friend or someone you loved?

Yes   No

If no, why not?

We don't talk that way to friends because it ruins the relationship.

5. Are you willing to apologize to yourself?

If yes, Self, apologize to your Self for....

6. Are you willing to forgive yourself?

7. What are 2-3 specific steps can you take to commit to doing better in this area?

Rejection

Rejection is a form of being hurt by others. To be rejected means that someone refuses to accept, consider, or receive you. We can be rejected by friends, parents, siblings, lovers, co-workers, etc. I've been rejected by co-workers, spiritual leaders, family members, and friends over the years. While rejection is a very normal part of relational experiences, being rejected can be extremely painful and can naturally cause you to doubt your worth and value. You can begin to doubt your ability to be a good son, daughter, friend, or spouse when someone you care for treats you with disregard. Being rejected is especially painful when you feel like you have been caring, open, and honest in the relationship.

Traumatic Experiences

Trauma is any difficult or unpleasant experience that causes someone to have mental or emotional problems. Trauma can include experiences as seemingly simple as being kicked out of your friend group in fourth grade, being chased or attacked by a dog, or tripping and falling in front of the whole school at an assembly (maybe all of these things have happened to me). Other times, trauma can look like being physically, emotionally, or verbally abused by a friend or family member, the death of a loved one, or losing a home to fire or bankruptcy. The level of trauma is not just measured by the experience, it is measured by the impact it makes in the life of the person.

It is really important for us to define trauma because it can include a wide range of experiences and ultimately includes a loss of something significant. An experience that causes trauma for one person may not cause trauma for someone else. Why? Because everyone is different. In my professional work, I find that most people underestimate the impact of their experiences on their mental, emotional, physical, and spiritual well-being. I am saying all of this to encourage you to be more open and curious about yourself and your experiences.

One of my most painful experiences with rejection was in a dating relationship. When I was almost 16 years old, I met a guy and literally fell in love with him at first sight. He was new to my school, so I got his attention by pretending to think he was someone else and repeatedly yelling the wrong name at him. It worked! He asked for my number, and we started talking on the phone at night and hanging out a little at school. I invited him to join me and my youth group on a trip to an amusement park as our first "date" and he agreed. Spending the whole day together was a whole new level for my 16-year-old self. After one roller coaster ride we were walking around the park holding hands, standing close, and making each other laugh all day long. Near the end of the day, I remember sitting near a fountain with him as we waited for everyone else. He just kept staring at me with such an intensity that it made me slightly uncomfortable. I laughed aloud and looked away. He kept staring. I widened my eyes at him as to say, "What?" He said, "You really have sexy lips." I blushed and said in my head, "Why don't you taste them!"

Listen, I was a fast-tale girl back in those days! He wasn't so fast. He didn't kiss me that day. Instead, he sat beside me on the van ride home, held my hand, and kissed it repeatedly like we were in some movie. I was on cloud nine! I say all of this because it was my first major attachment. I had dated many guys before him but when he entered my life, it felt different. We spent the next six months getting to know each other and one another's friends and families. We talked every day, hung out most days, took road trips, went to the movies, all the fun stuff that couples do. He was a bit of a late bloomer so it took about three months before we shared our first kiss. We spent a lot of time together but didn't have a "title" for our relationship.

At the six month point, I definitely wanted our relationship to be exclusive. I spent all of my time with him and wasn't really interested in being with anyone else.

Right around that time, another guy started showing some interest in me. He was very handsome and seemed super sweet. So I did what any decent girl would do. I told the guy I had been kissing and hanging out with for months that we needed to talk. He came to my house after school one day and I sat him down and simply asked him if he considered us to be dating or not. What he told me knocked the wind right out of my chest. He said, "No we are not dating. I don't do that. You are cool and all, but I am not into that."

I felt like I had been punched in my chest. He flat out rejected me, and I didn't even see it coming. I was devastated and didn't talk to him for several months. Eventually, he apologized, and we ended up dating for three years. But in hindsight, I noticed something about myself. After he rejected me, I felt so insecure in my dating relationships that I *always* kept a side piece. That rejection made me subconsciously believe that perhaps I wasn't good enough for someone to commit to. I thought that even if I truly loved someone, they could find a reason not to love me back. That belief kept me in a constant state of entertaining other love interests as side pieces.

It wasn't until I was in my 20's and started dating the man I am married to now, that I recognized my behavior of constantly dating or emotionally entertaining multiple men at once was rooted in the spirit of rejection. I questioned my ability to be monogamous, so I believed the lie that marriage would not be a good fit for me. I had difficulty being single-minded in my emotional commitment because I feared that I would dedicate so much time and effort into building intimacy with one person, only to learn that they did not want to be in a serious relationship with me.

On the surface, that may seem over-simplified. How does being "rejected" by someone you eventually ended up dating for three years translate into a spirit of rejection that became a stronghold in your emotional life? This is why understanding yourself, your story, and your trauma is important. Things are not always as they appear.

So my relationship with rejection did not begin with being rejected in a "situation-ship" at age 16, it started with my parents' divorce when I was 9 years old. My parents were married for 10 years, and it was rocky to say the least. But when you are a child, your parents are your parents, and your home is just home. You don't fully understand the context. Once my mother decided to end the relationship with my dad, she moved my three siblings and I to a community four hours away. At first, my dad visited a few weekends a month, continued to cook our meals, and spent time with us before heading back to our old city. But after a while, he just stopped. He didn't just stop visiting, he stopped calling too. He didn't respond to my letters and I didn't hear anything from him at all for three years. Once he finally reached out, there was no explanation or apology. My young heart was crushed. I

Valuing Yourself

not only felt rejected, I felt abandoned. I was popular in school, made strong grades, and had good friends, but I had an underlying feeling of wanting to belong to someone again. More specifically, I wanted a guy to see me, know me, and accept me. That's something I craved deeply.

I dated a lot when I was very young, but no one really stuck. I found myself either obsessed with one or two older guys who were attracted to me but didn't take me seriously, or being chased or smothered by some dude that was cute but not interesting to me.

When I connected with the new guy at 16, everything was different. He was my first strong male attachment since my dad abandoned and rejected me. So, when I finally felt like I belonged to someone and our feelings were mutual, being rejected again really did a number on my psyche. The feelings of rejection sent me into new modes of self-protection without me ever realizing it.

When I finally saw the spirit of rejection for what it was in my 30's, I was able to call it out, cry out to the Father for healing and come out of agreement with that spirit. Rejection tries to rear its ugly head from time to time and when it does, I've learned how to identify it quickly. In my life, the spirit of rejection can cause me to act in ways that are not consistent with my true self in order to avoid pain in relationships. This includes behaviors like people pleasing, fixing, ignoring character issues, or tolerating unacceptable behaviors.

When I say dealing with the "spirit" of rejection, I am referring to confronting any beliefs or mindsets I am entertaining that do not align with God's truth. Identifying a spirit of rejection and "casting" it out or down is not enough. We also have to tend to the emotional wound through things like worship, reflection, journaling prayer, coaching or counseling. In order to heal properly, we need to allow ourselves to feel our feelings and invite God into that experience.

Today, I am able to walk in healing knowing that when people reject me my value is not diminished. I don't need to fight, defend, or protect myself. Why? Because people coming or going out of my life does not increase or decrease my value. It is simply an experience that I can learn and grow from. Does it still hurt when people leave or reject me? Yes, at times. It may hurt me, but it doesn't change me. I've come to realize that sometimes people can't love and accept themselves so how can they truly love and accept you? The situations where men in my life chose to reject me were not really about me, it was about them. It was about who they were and where they were at the time. As a part of my healing process, I was able to find healthy ways to express the hurt, learn to forgive, and move forward with my life. These are three valuable skills that have helped me navigate emotional pain successfully time and time again. Allowing those relationships to change and evolve into alignment with God's plan set my life on a new course. I've come to accept that God allowed these men to reject me so that He could protect me.

Sometimes we experience trauma in relationships. When we are deeply hurt by others, we may feel less valuable and devalued. In 95% of cases, abuse of any kind is perpetuated by someone that a person knows. It's one thing to be harmed by a stranger. (Southwest Family Advocacy Center) It's another thing for those coarse words, violent actions, or inappropriate/unwanted advances to come from someone who knows you. They may have grown up in the home with you, slept beside you each night, or shared the same friends. When we know the person who hurt us, it's a bit more personal. Subconsciously, we may question whether we had done something wrong, deserved it, or if we were just overreacting.

If you've struggled with a situation like this it's important for you to know that what was done to you was **wrong** and you did not deserve that. Even if someone made the decision to disrespect you, that choice is a reflection of their character, **not your value.** Be careful not to make decisions about your value based on someone else's shortcomings. What happened **to** you does not define you. Your experiences are not the essence of who you are, your value is. Reject the idea that the person hurt you because you did not deserve to be treated any better. You are not worthless! You are worthy of being treated with respect. Accept the truth that hurt people hurt people. Declare that this situation will make you better, not bitter. You have the power to process your pain and rewrite your narrative. You are an overcomer!

I will briefly share some common issues that open the door to rejection.

Charter Issues.

Character can be defined as a collection of personality traits within our behavior that shows who we are. Charter is who we are when no one is watching. Christian charter is a choice and is always under development as we submit to Christ and are empowered by the Holy Spirit. Character issues are simply any of the ways we behave that align with the works of the flesh over the fruit of the spirit.

The works of the flesh versus the fruit of the Spirit are explained in Galatians 5:19-21:

> *"When you follow the desires of your sinful nature, the results are very clear: sexual immorality, impurity, lustful pleasures, idolatry, sorcery, hostility, quarreling,*

> *jealousy, outbursts of anger, selfish ambition, dissension, division, envy, drunkenness, wild parties, and other sins like these. Let me tell you again, as I have before, that anyone living that sort of life will not inherit the Kingdom of God. But the Holy Spirit produces this kind of fruit in our lives: love, joy, peace, patience, kindness, goodness, faithfulness, gentleness, and self-control. There is no law against these things!"*

Despite our intrinsic value, we are still a work in progress. Sometimes we behave in ways that can cause others to move away from us because of charter issues in our own lives. If you lack self-awareness or struggle with pride in an attempt to protect your ego, you may be unable to see yourself. People can also reject you for having Godly character. This can be especially true if your moral charter rises above the baseline of a specific relationship or a friend group. Sometimes others are not ready to embrace the charter changes that God has called you to. When this happens, you may find yourself suddenly incompatible with people who were once close to you. While this can be painful, it is necessary. Everyone needs time and space to grow in their relationship with God and themselves at an authentic pace. Sometimes this will require distance or detachment in relationships for a season or maybe even a lifetime.

Other times, the charter issue is not yours, the problem is someone else's charter. Remember, people are people. In the same way we struggle with charter issues, others do as well. If someone in your life struggles with sin patterns or habits like lying, cheating, stealing, or dishonesty, it is not uncommon for them to move away from you, especially if you are opposed to the choices they are making.

Conflict

Rejection can show up when there is conflict. Conflict is a clash between individuals arising out of a difference in thought process, attitudes, perceptions, understanding, interests, and requirements. When the issue can be resolved, it's more common for people to be able to smooth things over and continue relationships. When a conflict cannot be resolved, it may require a change or ending of the relationship.

Many times people experience rejection due to conflict that could not be resolved in a relationship. In these situations, it's important to understand that when conflict occurs, it is natural and normal for our relationships to change and maybe even end. When we do not process the emotional pain and work to accept this truth, we can begin to internalize deep feelings of unworthiness as a result of the people we love turning away from us. We may struggle with thoughts like "We were so close, and they knew me so well. If they don't want me anymore, I must really be worthless." Please note, this is a lie from the pit of Hell. Not all relationships last forever, even the ones we value most. God's love for us makes healing from lost relationships possible.

Misalignment

Rejection can show up when there is misalignment. Misalignment is the condition of being out of correct position or improperly aligned. (Das 2023) As a follower of Jesus, everything in our lives is about alignment; correct positioning and proper alignment to the will of the Father! Accepting Jesus is free but following Him will cost you everything, relationships included. Relationships are a major currency in the kingdom of God. As we read the bible, we see countless examples of how God uses people, places, and his plan to shift His people out of ordinary, everyday life into the purpose and destiny He created them for. Some of the loss or rejection you experience may not be due to conflict or an error on someone's part. At times, we simply become misaligned in relationships, and it is time to let go. To truly follow Jesus means that we must be willing to let go of anything or anyone to stay in step with His way and His plan for our lives. I've learned how to process these experiences as an opportunity to release so that I can receive God's best for me for what is ahead. Accepting misalignment and the sense of rejection that can come with it is truly an invitation to trust God, His sovereignty, and His time.

If you get the sense that you were really being a good and kind person and someone rejected you, it can feel like an assault on your personhood. If you think you may be struggling with feelings of rejection in a relationship, you may want to ask yourself some of the questions below.

Reflection Questions

1. Is there anything I did or said to warrant not being accepted?

2. Was my behavior or speech consistent with my authentic self?

3. Am I being rejected because of what the other person thinks or feels?

4. Do I really know how they think or feel or am I just making assumptions?

5. Have I shared my feelings with another person?

6. Is it safe and appropriate to share my feelings in this situation?

7. Have I prayed about this situation and asked God for insight and guidance?

As long as you are loved and accepted by God, you have enough to keep moving forward. His love for you is enough. Always enough.

CHAPTER 4

Embracing Your Strength

Everyone has strengths, Everyone. That includes you. Your strengths do not make you better than anyone, they are a part of what makes you, you. Strengths are God's gift to you, and they compliment your God given assignment, purpose, and calling. In this chapter, we will define strength, explore God's word on the topic, and pursue embracing it more fully.

What are strengths?

Strengths are positive character traits or skills related to someone's personal character or tasks/actions they can do well. Strengths can include knowledge, attributes, skills, and talents. (Davis n.d.) Because we are multidimensional beings, I believe we can have strengths in the different parts of who we are; mentally, physically, emotionally, spiritually, and more. Knowing and accepting your personal strengths is a vital part of knowing and accepting yourself. Your strengths are one component of your personality. Your personality is a major component of your identity.

Let's take Delilah, for example. Delilah was Samson's love interest from the Valley of Sorek (Judg. 16). Most of us are aware of Delilah's weakness. She was untrustworthy, a betrayer, and valued money more than relationships. All the while, Delilah also had great strength. In addition to being attractive, Delilah was persistent when faced with obstacles. Did Delilah have flaws? Sure.

Did she make poor choices? Absolutely. Although she is famous for her flaws, her flaws do not eliminate her strength.

How do you define yourself? Do you tend to focus on your flaws or mistakes? If the answer is yes, it's no surprise if you struggle or waiver in your feelings about yourself. If you hyper-focus on your weaknesses, you will constantly battle feelings of unworthiness, discomfort, and self-loathing.

If you are aware of your weakness but choose to lean in on your strength, you will experience a greater sense of acceptance, grace, self-love, and compassion.

Let me show you how.

In the bible, there is a lot of information about people's personalities, to include their strengths, weaknesses, abilities, character, and much more. Every person mentioned in the scriptures has value and personal strengths. Every person. Even the people who used, abused, manipulated, and controlled others to get their own way. They all had personal strengths.

Delilah deceived Samson, but she was persistent.
Eli ignored sin, but he was faithful to Israel.
David was a murderer, yet he was a man after God's own heart.
King Saul was emotionally immature, yet he was generous.
Judas was a trader, and he left everything to follow Jesus.
Ahab was an evil king, and he was a strategist.
Jezebel was a controlling, pagan worshiper but she was strong.
Pharaoh ignored God, but he was a strong leader.
Satan was greedy and prideful and he was beautiful.

Every single person has value despite their weaknesses.
Even you.
Your personal strengths are connected to the innate value God has placed inside of you. You don't have to be the best at something

or better than someone else to have value or strength, you just have to be you. Be who you are, where you are, right here, right now.

I find that most people who struggle with self-esteem spend a lot of time looking up to other people and looking down on themselves. Comparison is a trap! There is enough space on the Earth for both you and someone else to have strengths and be great at the same time! I cancel the lie from the enemy that you are not good enough because you don't have the same gifts, talents, abilities, or skill set as _____ (You fill in the blank, you know who you compare yourself to). Just stop it! Let's call comparison what it really is, foolishness. It is natural for children to compare themselves to others because that is how they learn and grow. But here's the thing, you are no longer a child. If you find your adult self still comparing and contrasting yourself to other people, now is the time to level up and discover a pathway to self-acceptance and self-love.

> "When I was a child, I spoke like a child, I thought like a child, I reasoned like a child. When I became a man, I gave up childish ways." (1 Cor. 13:1)

Let me show you how to elevate your thinking about strengths and comparison.

Why You Should Embrace Your Strengths

Strengths are God's gift to you, and they complement your God given assignment, purpose, and calling. Your strengths are assigned to you to equip you to fulfill your calling. Not *her* calling or *his* calling, **your** calling. If you have found yourself questioning why you do not look, act, function, or flow like someone else, this is your answer. You do not have someone else's strength because you are not called to their calling, you are called to yours! This is why comparison is such a dead end. When you get the revelation that God has placed *good* things inside of you to fulfill your unique calling in the Earth, when comparison shows up you will not entertain it. It is time to mature in our God given identity. Accepting our strengths can help us do just that.

Right now, you might be like, "Rosa, you're preaching real good sis! But tell me something, how can I actually embrace my strengths?"

Embracing Your Strengths

We embrace our God given strengths through three actions: identification, acknowledgment, and acceptance.

Identify Your Strengths

The first step to embracing your strengths is to identify them. How can you embrace something that you are unaware of or unfamiliar with? You cannot. Whenever I begin a coaching or counseling relationship with someone one of the first things I assess is awareness of personal strengths. Why? Because people who can recognize the good in themselves are generally healthy and self-aware. People who struggle to see their own strengths are most likely wrestling with low self-esteem. One of my early interventions is to help people see the good in themselves and accept that good because **the way you think and feel about yourself is the filter for your entire life.** "As a man thinks, so is he." (Prov. 23:7)

How's Your Filter?

In the space below, make a list of your top 25 personal strengths. Do not ask anyone. Simply complete this task independently. Please do this without judgment or shame. Just make a list. If you are not able to list 25 strengths, no worries, you will be able to add more over time.

My Top 25 Strengths

Reflection Question

1. How well do I know my strengths?

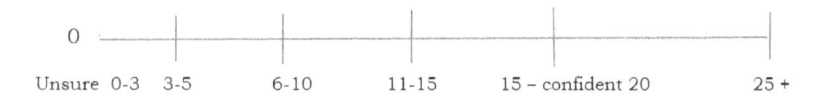

```
0 ─────┼──────────┼──────────┼──────────┼──────────┤
Unsure 0-3   3-5      6-10       11-15    15 – confident 20    25 +
```

2. What does my current level of awareness say about me?

3. Do you have feelings of guilt or shame about this list? Why or why not? Joy or pride?

4. Is there something I need to ask God for help with concerning my ability to see myself in my strength?

Every now and then return to your strengths list. Sit with your Self and the Holy Spirit to see if there is a strength you need to add. As God heals, grows, and matures us we *increase* in strength, skills, abilities, and talents.

For example, before the age of 30 I could not cook. It was pretty bad. I married in my early 20's and my husband was well aware of my limitations in this area. Once we started having children, I believe God gave me a desire to become a good cook as a way of serving my children. I wanted to make food that my children wanted to eat and feel good about sharing with others. I desired to express my love through my cooking.

So, I set out to learn how to cook. I had many women around me who could cook and bake very well, and I had been eating their food for years. I simply started by asking them for recipes, cooking them, and sharing my food with people I trusted to give me honest feedback. Over the course of five years, my ability to cook went from a weakness to a strength! Now my friends and family ask me to cook dishes for them and I share recipes regularly.

Types of Strengths

There are many different types of strengths. Strengths are just as multidimensional as we are. In the exercise Below, I have developed a vast list of strengths from a multidimensional perspective. Review the list below and check any strengths that you feel may apply to you:

STRENGTHS FINDER

Adaptable
Affectionate
Ambitious
Articulate
Aspiring
Calm
Candid
Capable
Caring
Charismatic
Cheerful
Clear headed
Communicative
Competitive
Considerate
Cooperative
Courageous
Courteous
Creative
Curious
Decisive
Determined
Devoted
Diligent
Efficient
Empathetic
Endures
Energetic
Enthusiastic
Expansive
Experienced

Flexible
Focused
Forgiving
Forthright
Frank
Friendly
Generous
Grateful
Hard-working
Helpful
Honest
Humble
Imaginative
Independent
Innovative
Insightful
Intuitive
Inventive
Involved
Kind
Mature
Methodical
Meticulous
Modest
Motivated
Natural leader
Neat
Objective
Open minded
Optimistic
Organized

Outspoken
Painstaking
Passionate
Patient
Perceptive
Perseveres
Persuasive
Polite
Practical
Proactive
Prudent
Punctual
Realistic
Reliable
Resourceful
Respectful
Responsible
Responsive
Seasoned
Self-confident
Self-directed
Self-disciplined
Self-reliant
Selfless
Sensible
Serious
Sincere
Sociable
Sympathetic
Systematic

(Mead 2020)

Embracing Your Strength

Take a look at all of the strengths you checked off on the list above. Select the five strengths you identify with the most. Write them down below and write a few sentences to reflect on each one.

Stength #1:

Stength #2:

Stength #3:

Stength #4:

Stength #5:

Identifying your strengths should be a life-long journey and practice that keeps you aligned with yourself and your God. Hebrews 13:8 says that God never changes, He is the same yesterday, today, and forever. (Heb. 13:8)

While God stays that same– we change. We will grow, evolve, and shift until we see Him face to face, at which time we will be like Him. Until then, it's important that we keep a pulse on ourselves. Once we've gone through the initial process of identifying our strengths, it's time to acknowledge them.

Acknowledging Your Strengths

Identifying your strengths is not enough, you must also acknowledge them. Let's say you've been friends with someone for several years. You consider them to be someone you are close to and care a lot about. When you are in large social gatherings, it's pretty easy for you to identify them based on their height, hair color, the way they dress, the sound of their voice, etc. But what if you just stopped there? What if you identified your friend, but you didn't acknowledge them. You looked them dead in the face, maybe even made eye contact but you didn't wave, offer a friendly smile, or even a head nod. If you didn't acknowledge this friend, how would that impact the relationship?

Most likely, your friend would feel left out, ignored, rejected, invisible, disrespected, hurt, or disappointed. Well, my friend, you are a whole person, and you are in a relationship with your Self. If you are not able to acknowledge your strengths, you may leave your Self feeling left out, ignored, rejected, invisible, disrespected, hurt, or disappointed. Isn't that something? I wonder how many times we have experienced some of these negative emotions due to our inability to acknowledge ourselves and possibly blamed it on others.

Sometimes the emotional and/or spiritual pain and discomfort we feel is self-inflicted. If you can't acknowledge your strengths, you won't feel very good about yourself, and you will struggle with emotional resilience. To recognize your strengths simply means to acknowledge the existence, validity, or legality of it. We acknowledge our strengths by giving ourselves an internal wave, smile, or nod to confirm that it exists. Such actions are a way of creating space for your authentic self to show up, take up space, and shine through. Strengths are not to be covered up and it's okay for them to be displayed. After all, our shine produces light that allows people to be drawn to us so we can point them toward Jesus.

> *"You are the light of the world. A city set on a hill cannot be hidden.Nor do people light a lamp and put it under a basket, but on a stand, and it gives light to all in the house. In the same way, let your light shine before others, so that*[a] they may see your good works and give glory to your Father who is in heaven."* (Matt. 15:14-16)

The ways that God causes us to shine are tools for evangelism that advance the kingdom of God and His plan for all of creation! Did you catch it? Your strengths are part of God's master plan to restore all of creation back to Himself.

Accepting Your Strengths

Once you identify your strengths and acknowledge them, the next step is acceptance. Acceptance is the action of consenting to receive or undertake something offered. Emotionally, acceptance is a process of *receiving ourselves* as adequate or suitable. God has given you strengths and planted them inside of you to fulfill your purpose and His plan on the Earth. His words are true. According to 2 Corinthians 4:7, *"But we have this treasure in jars of clay, to show that the surpassing power belongs to God and not to us."* God has placed value in you.

The question is not whether or not the strengths are there, the question is whether or not you will accept them?

Rediscovering You

Reflection Questions

1. Will you accept your God-given strengths?

    Yes   No   Unsure

2. If you have been struggling in your ability to see your strength, worth, or value, do you give the Holy Spirit *consent* to access your heart and mind? He can help to remove any thoughts or ideas that hinder you from accepting your God-given design. List 2-3 specific actions or steps can you take to give him access?

    1._____

    2._____

    3._____

3. Even if you wrestle or struggle with accepting your strengths, can you *receive* them *by faith* as a gift from your Heavenly Father? Not as a reward for something you have done. Not something given to you out of pity, but *receiving* your strengths as a loving gift from your Heavenly Father? Yes or No

4. Below, write out 3-5 scriptures that remind you to receive God's gift to you by faith.

    Scripture 1:_____

    Scripture 2:_____

Scripture 3:_____

Scripture 4:_____

Scripture 5:_____

You see, God already received you. *"But God demonstrates his own love for us, in this; while we were still sinners, Christ died for us."* (Rom. 5:8)

Maybe it's time for you to get in agreement with God and receive yourself? To receive yourself means to accept yourself and your strengths. It's time for you to receive yourself as adequate and suitable.

You are adequate.

You are enough.

You are suitable.

You are sufficient.

You are appropriate for your assignment.

You are right for this situation.

Truth be told, everyone struggles with feelings of inadequacy or unworthiness from time to time. People who say they never struggle with these feelings are most likely living a very safe life that is beneath their actual calling or really struggling to navigate their emotional selves. If you are truly pursuing God's plan for your life you **should** feel inadequate at times. Having strengths does not make you perfect, all powerful, or all knowing. Only God is those things. Feelings of inadequacy will arise if you are truly pursuing God's will. We serve a BIG God whose plans are bigger than our capacity, so it is completely normal for feelings of inadequacy to arise. Apart from him, we can do nothing (John 15:5).

The pathway to embracing your strengths is not about never feeling small or inadequate again, it's about recognizing, owning, and receiving the power that God has placed in you and living from that place of awareness and ability every single day.

Strengths should cause you to lift up your head, walk in the light of God's glory and be unashamed. There are plenty of struggles and trials in this life, don't allow the gift of your strengths to become a burden instead of a blessing.

Reflection Prayer

Thank you for my strengths of _____, _____, _____, _____, _____. Thank you for the new strengths that you will reveal to me in the days ahead. I confess anything that I think or believe that stops me from identifying, recognizing, and accepting my strengths. I destroy arguments and every lofty opinion raised against the knowledge of God and take every thought captive to obey Christ. God has placed value in me and thinks good thoughts toward me. I accept my strengths now because I have the mind of Christ. Please help me stand against fear and doubt. I open my heart to your healing, my mind to your restoration, and my will to your will. Have your way in me. Strengthen me for your purposes. In Jesus' name, Amen.

CHAPTER 5

Embracing Your Weakness

If strengths are positive character traits or attributes related to someone's personal character, are weaknesses just the opposite? I argue that most of us define weakness as our negative character traits. Defining weakness as "negativity" is an oversimplification of what our weaknesses are and the purpose they serve. Once again, I am inviting you to leave elementary thinking and oversimplification behind.

By definition, weakness is the state or condition of lacking strength. Many times, weaknesses are qualities or features regarded as a disadvantage or fault. (Collins English Dictionary 2005)

In regard to behavior, sometimes weakness is referred to as a person having difficulty or resisting something or someone. When I ask people to tell me their strengths, they freeze up like a deer in headlights. When I ask people to tell me their weaknesses, the answer comes rushing from their lips like water from a faucet. I usually have to ask them to stop sharing.

Why is this? Why are we so fixated on our deficiencies? Being fixated on your weakness is a trick of the enemy of your soul. Whatever you fixate on drives the thoughts, feelings, behaviors, and circumstances that make up your life. In other words, if you are hyper-focused on your weakness, you will be limited and weak.

Hyper-focusing on our weakness steals your strength and joy. Ignoring our weakness steals your wisdom and insight. Our goal is to help you be aware of your weaknesses and use them as a tool instead of a weapon. When we understand our weaknesses and submit them under God's authority, He can use your weakness for your good and for His glory.

Weakness and the Bible

Weakness is a hot topic in God's word. Anyone who has read the bible is aware of the character deficiencies of the great men & women of God. Consider King David. David was a shepherd boy who was chosen by God to be the King of Israel. David's strengths included being handsome, hardworking, courageous, a talented musician, a resilient warrior, a worshiper, a faithful friend, and much more. One of the highest compliments that David received in the scripture is that he was "a man after God's own heart" (Acts 13:22)

On the contrary, David had a number of weaknesses and charter flaws that included: lying, dishonesty, lust, murderer, disobedience, and a lax/absent father to his own children. "King David was a man of contrast. At times he was single–minded and devoted to God, yet at other times he failed miserably, committing some of the most serious sins recorded in the Old Testament." (Zavada 2018)

Much like King David, you are a person of contrasts. At times you may be deeply devoted to God, yet at other times you will fail miserably.

"In some ways, we are all modern day King Davids. Thriving in strengths and wrestling with weaknesses, all to the glory of God. Notice King David's story didn't end with him committing adultery with Bathsheba, sending Uriah to war –to be killed, or ignoring God's command not to take a census of the people. He went on to discover a truth that would restore his soul and give his life purpose and direction again; we see that truth revealed in the Book of Psalm.. Psalm is a beautiful book written by King David. It is a collection of prayers, poetry and worship that recounts Israel's history + God's covenant promises. "The Psalms help us to know that we are not the first to feel God is silent when we pray, nor are we the first to feel immense anguish and bewilderment in prayer or intense emotions in life." (Elliott 2018)

Our weaknesses and limitations are a normal part of our humanity and do not rob us of value. Because we are in a broken and fallen world, none of us get to be perfect, only God is perfect. Our weaknesses are a reminder of our need for God's power and strength in our lives. Having limitations is not a problem. Our problems set in when we do not respect our limits. The world has a basic standard that says having weakness makes you weak. To be weak is to be devalued and you should be ashamed. My friend, this is not God's standard.

This is a worldly standard.

The Kingdom of God uses weakness as a portal for God's glory to be revealed.

The world says, "Weak people have no power or strength."

God says, *"For when I am weak, I am strong."* (2 Cor. 12:10)

The world says, "Weak people are limited."

God says, *"I can do all things through Christ who strengthens me."* (Phil. 4:13)

The world says, "Things will always be this way. It will not get better for you."

God says, "*And after you have suffered a little while, the God of all grace, who has called you to his eternal glory in Christ, will himself restore, confirm, strengthen, and establish you.*" (1 Peter 5:10)

The world says, "The weak are losers who never win!"

God says, "*The last shall be first and the first shall be last.*" (Matt. 20:16)

Whose report will you believe?

The Truth About Weakness

Authentic emotional and spiritual health require a mindset shift that normalizes weakness and limitations as a normal and necessary expression of our humanity and journey as a follower of Jesus. Here are just a few truths that I want to recap about weakness before we move forward. When you find yourself struggling to let go of the guilt, shame, and self-judgment that accompanies your weaknesses/limitations, these are a few truths to help bring you back to reality. You may want to store this list in your phone or a journal where you can easily access them.

1. All people have weaknesses/limitations, myself included.

2. Having weaknesses does not make me weak, unworthy, or less than others.

3. Having weaknesses makes me human.

4. My weaknesses keep me partnered with God and the Holy Spirit.

5. My weaknesses are an integral part of God's plan, purpose, and design.

6. My weakness is a place of empowerment.

7. Embracing my weakness is part of embracing myself.

What I love most about accepting my weaknesses is the liberation and freedom it brings, especially once you learn how to work with it and not against it.

I have my fair share of weaknesses, including: impatience, vanity, verbal aggression, and pride, just to name a few. I used to experience deep levels of shame connected to these weaknesses but with some inner healing work and God's help, I am growing in grace in these areas and learning to be much more accepting of myself. I will share about one of these areas, after all, I can't put *all* of my business in the street!

Let's talk about verbal aggression. I am a passionate person with strong communication skills. When I get upset about something, my natural reaction is to get excited, elevate my voice, and maybe even express anger or some other strong emotion I am feeling. There is nothing wrong with feeling anger, as the bible teaches us that we can be angry but sin not (Eph. 4:26). Often times, my anger will turn into sin when I lash out at people by using verbal aggression. Like others who struggle with this issue, I use verbal aggression to control people and situations. Sometimes I am conscious of my behavior and other times I am not. Regardless of my level of consciousness, the choice to use my words to dominate and control people and things is a poor choice.

I didn't really become aware of how much of an issue this was until I started taking on greater levels of leadership in business and ministry. I am a growth-oriented person, so I routinely ask for feedback from my teammates as a way to learn and grow. During a particular season, I received consistent feedback from people in different settings about my non-verbal and verbal communication when tensions got high, or someone was not meeting my expectations.

I became more curious and asked the persons who provided the feedback how my actions made them feel and impacted our relationship. The responses were not at all aligned with my heart's intention as a leader and follower of Jesus. It was then that I decided things needed to change. I got more serious about observing myself and my communication, especially under stress and pressure. I realized a few things about myself. First, I am a very fast-paced person. I like to complete tasks and check off my boxes. While that serves me well in lots of areas, moving quickly is not always wise when dealing with people and communication.

I learned that I sometimes tend to put processes and projects before people, so when things move too slowly, I get frustrated and communicate with anger. Specifically, I noticed myself using aggression to make people experience the discomfort I was feeling so they could snap out of it. The anger/aggression worked in the moment, but had negative long-term effects, including decreased feelings of intimacy, safety, unity, and collaboration. I found this impact to be true in my personal and professional relationships.

Now that I am more self-aware in the area of communication, I have learned how to move differently. I navigate my weakness by doing things like:

*Giving myself time to fully process my emotions before I react or respond to people.

*Making a conscious effort to be gracious, even if someone else is being disrespectful or dishonoring me.

*Searching for win-win situations in conflict resolution.

*Practicing what I will say before having critical conversations with others.

*Remaining mindful of my tone of voice and facial expressions during communication.

*Practicing active listening and remaining curious instead of being judgmental.

I don't always get this right; I am definitely a work in progress. But I have learned to embrace my imperfection and enjoy the journey.

Once you get to the place where you can be honest with yourself about your weakness, you can open yourself up to receive something new that God has for you. God has a way of teaching, training, and refining us. One of the ways we lend ourselves to that process is accepting our weaknesses and not hiding them.

Your weaknesses are not a curse, they are actually a gift that keeps giving.

When you can accept your weakness you can experience:

- **Greater self-awareness.** When you are honest about your weaknesses, you open yourself up to the empowerment needed to heal, grow, and/or change.

- **Open yourself to practice self-comparison.** Accepting the not-so-glamorous parts of yourself takes some *real* courage and *deep* self-love. Accepting your weaknesses in a healthy way is an invitation for you to learn how to come alongside yourself and be a better friend to your Self. Many of us are great friends to others but when it comes to our Self, the grace is nowhere to be found. You deserve to receive from yourself just as much compassion as you give to others.

- **Increased grace for other flawed humans.** Learning how to be loving and accepting of yourself despite your weaknesses requires an expansion in your heart and mind. When we learn how to be more emotionally flexible and supportive in our relationship with our Self, we find more love and grace available to extend to others.

- **Learn how to partner with God instead of relying too much on self or others.** God knows all about our weaknesses. He placed them there for a reason. Our weaknesses are a reminder of our desperate need for the Father. As we embrace them, we turn to him and ask Him to be strong in our weakness. As we grow in this way, we learn that all of the balls are *not* in our court and we do not have to do everything in our own strength. We learn to release control and allow certain things to be undone until God gets to it. We do not have anything to prove, and we are not responsible for fixing everything.

- **Ask God for help in prayer.** Accepting our weaknesses helps to keep us postured in prayer. My simple prayer in weakness is, "Lord, I cannot, you can." Asking God for help is an act of surrender that we should continually practice.

- **Make better decisions.** Understanding and accepting your weakness is a great way to stay connected to reality. Some people ignore their weakness and make decisions that are not consistent with what is true. We know that God can do all things and we have a responsibility to steward all things well. Knowing your weaknesses/limitations can help you make wise choices without fear.

Do you want this for your life? I certainly do! There is something that really gets in the way of us accepting ourselves in this way. Let's take a look at this barrier before I teach you how to go for it!

The Perfectionist Mindset

The Perfectionist Mindset is rooted in the belief that your self-worth is based on your achievements. Unless you are just now showing up to this party, you already know that this mindset if false! What is your self-worth is based on? The answer is "my identity as a son or daughter of God" or "my identity in Christ". If you got that incorrect, please stop here and go back to the beginning of this book send me a private message for some prayer… lol!

Most professionals link the perfectionist mindset to personality types. While I agree that certain personality types are more prone to this type of thinking, we all can be victims to it for a number of reasons. Western culture has a major emphasis on joy, happiness, pleasure, and instant gratification.

The western world is filled with performance-based church cultures, technological advances, robust business/industry, and freedoms of many kinds. As a result, many Westerners have high expectations about how they should be experiencing life. Christians in the Western world are no exception to this rule. How so?

We expect things to be clean, organized, and beautiful. When they are not, we are well aware of how this negatively impacts our mood and productivity. We expect people to be respectful and civil. When they are not, we start social movements, campaigns, and create laws to support this standard of respect. We expect to have things our way, right away. When they are not, we complain or file a lawsuit. In western culture, most things that once included long processes are expedited through turbo car washes, fast food, instant pay, or food deliveries. There is no need to wait.

The problem with instant gratification is that it skips the process. The process, while slow, is a way of engaging in life that leads to learning, growth, and character development. Many people achieve temporary happiness, pleasure, and gratification, but their lives are not transformed. Why? Because they have not been processed. The place where people *become* is called *The Process.* People are made in the process. If you want to let go of the Perfectionist Mindset start letting your *"Yes"* to the process serve as a *"No"* to Perfectionism. #processoverprofection.

Well, Rosa, how do you know that their lives are not being transformed?

People with a perfectionist mindset are **never** satisfied. Perfection is not obtainable so when perfection is the goal, nothing is never good enough. People with this mindset moan, groan, and complain about what they lack. They may not do it aloud, but they do it in their hearts and their heads. They may even pray about it. Maybe God opens a door and makes a way. Perhaps they accomplish something in their own strength. As a counselor/coach, naturally you get exiled! Surely, seeing what they were able to accomplish or how God made a way is enough to set them free from the mental and emotional torment they were experiencing? Only, it doesn't.

They are not able to use the experience to build their faith. It's filtered as a moment of gratification, and they find something else that is not *just so* to fixate on and start the exhausting process all over again. It's all so exhausting. I know because I am a recovering perfectionist. I used to be one of *those people*. In a moment of weakness, I can find myself in that struggle and feeling exhausted.

If we find ourselves leaning toward perfection more often than not, we really need to check our motives and core beliefs. Being perfect or getting everything "right" is not what pleases God.

> *"But without faith it is impossible to please him: for he that cometh to God must believe that he is, and that he is a rewarder of them that diligently seek him."* (Heb. 11:6)

When we seek perfection, we are focused on pleasing ourselves and others, not God. A person with a Perfectionist Mindset doesn't just lack confidence in themselves or the situation. They lack trust in God. They lack faith, and without faith it is impossible to please God (Heb. 11:6).

Social Media

Social Media has transformed the way we live. While some people appreciate and enjoy social media, others despise and demonize it. Personally, I liken social media to money; it is amoral–lacking a moral sense and unconcerned with the rightness or wrongness of something. The impact of social media on someone's life is based on how they choose to use it.

On the positive side, social media provides a convenient way to connect to our family members, friends, and relatives through pictures, video, and on-demand communication. In this way, social media can help us strengthen relationships and create new connections in a way that was not possible in the past.

On the flip side, engaging in social media can negatively impact your mental, spiritual, and emotional health through the comparison factor. "We fall into the trap of comparing ourselves to others as we scroll through our feeds, and make judgments about how we measure up. (Walton 2017)" What we see on social media is not always an indicator of how things really are in the world, it's just a reflection of what people choose to show us.

Managing Other People's Expectations

Let's be honest, some of us don't actually have a Perfectionist Mindset, but we live and/or work with someone who does. It may be your pastor, spouse, partner, boss, parent, friend, or child. And let's face it, no one wants to disappoint or fail someone they care about or are accountable to.

Here's the thing, if you don't have a perfectionist mindset, that's fantastic. It's one demon you don't have to fight. Be careful not to <u>act</u> or behave in ways that are inconsistent with what you believe; not for your pastor, your boss, your spouse, not for anyone! Some of us are running around striving to get everything just right because of the pressure you receive from someone else. If you find yourself functioning this way in any relationship, this is cause for pause and concern.

If you are trying to be perfect or make things *just so* for someone else, you may be headed toward a codependent relationship, if you're not already there. It is possible to love or care about a person without taking responsibility for managing their emotions. In situations like these, oftentimes the people pleaser is managing someone else's anxiety, worry, fear, doubt, compulsion, or sadness for them. People are responsible for managing their own emotions. You are responsible for showing distressed people empathy, compassion, and care, you are not responsible for managing their emotions.

If being in an authentic and equitable relationship with someone means they get to know you for who you really are. If you are not a perfectionist, you shouldn't act like one. If you don't know how to set appropriate boundaries with people who try to project their feelings on you it's time to level up in your communication skills. God created you to please Him, not people.

This may seem bold to some of you, but I want to challenge your thinking in this area. If you are bound up in people-pleasing you are coming into alignment with a spirit. It may seem simple, but as you manage the emotions of another who has a Perfectionist Mindset, you take on that belief system of bondage and spirit that comes with it, the spirit of rejection, fear, anger, and low self-worth. Some of you don't even have a perfectionist mindset but find yourself struggling with your self-esteem. If you set some healthy boundaries or break these attachments where possible, healing will manifest in the way that you think and feel about yourself. I speak that <u>now</u> in Jesus' name!

How To Embrace Your Weakness

It's strategy time! There are several ways for you to go about embracing your weakness, so let's get to it.

First, it's important to accept that all people have flaws, including you. I know I said this before but I need to repeat it again. Why? Because if you cannot accept the biblical truth that *all* have sinned and fallen short of the glory of God (Rom. 3:23) you can't break free.

If you find yourself resistant to this biblical truth, it's time to focus on getting truths inside of your heart and head so the chains of guilt, shame, and people- pleasing can break off of your life! See *Scriptures for Embracing My Weaknesses* in the Resource section in the back of this book. Read these scriptures aloud, meditate on them, memorize them, journal and write about them. Engage with them in whatever ways you need to until God's truth becomes your reality.

Just like we identified our strengths we will identify our weaknesses.

Reflection Questions

List your Top 10 Weaknesses or Limitations.

1.
2.
3.
4.
5.
6.
7.
8.
9.
10.

From the list above, write down the three weaknesses you struggle with the most. Write a brief reflection/description of each.

1.

2.

3.

Write out 3-5 scriptures you can read to encourage yourself when you are wrestling and/or being refined through your weaknesses/limitations. See *Scriptures for Embracing My Weaknesses* in the Resource section in the back of this book if you need some ideas.

1.
2.
3.
4.
5.

Recognize Your Limitations

Now that you've identified your limitations, it's time to **recognize** them. Remember, to recognize your limitations simply means to acknowledge the existence, validity, and legality of them. I can imagine some of you saying or thinking things like:

1. God is perfect, so should I strive to be perfect?

2. Does God want me to come into agreement with my weakness?

3. If I acknowledge my weakness, am I giving it more power over me?"

4. This sounds demonic. Weaknesses are a curse not a blessing. I am not coming into agreement with something negative over my life!

5. Recognizing my weakness means I am giving into sin and giving up on being like Jesus.

If you find yourself entertaining these thoughts or questions you are not alone. Many Christians think like this when it comes to wrestling with a complex issue like healthy self-esteem. The Church has invested so much time teaching us how to love, care for, respect, and honor others but has been mostly silent regarding how to love yourself well.

As a mental health professional and coach specializing in Christian counseling, the Christian's misuse and misunderstanding of the value and treatment of *Self* is both harmful and neglectful. If your heart and mind are aligned with the questions and statements I shared, you are dealing with some lies, often taught in the church, and they are holding you hostage.

I am not here to judge you. At some point I probably bought into some of this erroneous teaching, too. I am here to introduce you to a new way of thinking and believing supported by the scriptures. This pathway is one that I've used with my clients for many years and has led thousands of people to hope and healing. It is highly effective in helping people find a healthy way of seeing themselves for who they really are and choosing to love themselves despite what they see.

Why is this so important? Because that's what God does. He sees us fully as we are and accepts us just as we are.

> [13] *For you formed my inward parts; you knitted me together in my mother's womb.*

> *14 I praise you, for I am fearfully and wonderfully made. Wonderful are your works; my soul knows it very well.*
>
> *15 My frame was not hidden from you, when I was being made in secret, intricately woven in the depths of the earth.*
>
> *16 Your eyes saw my unformed substance; in your book were written, every one of them, the days that were formed for me, when as yet there was none of them.* (Ps. 139:13-16)

When we learn to follow His example in this, we'll be happier and healthier for ourselves and everyone around us.

Facing Illusions

I want us to circle back to a concept we discussed earlier. The enemy of your soul wants to make you believe that having a weakness makes you weak and less valuable. That is *not* what the word of God teaches us. Believing that a person who lacks strength has less value is a logical idea. It makes sense, right? People who are strong are valuable because they can achieve and accomplish more. People who lack strength or display weakness are less valuable because they can achieve or accomplish less than others.

We never actually say these statements aloud, do we? No, certainly not. But you don't have to say something aloud in order to be committed to it in your heart. Unfortunately, most Christians actually believe this. We never *say* it; but we *believe* it.

Rosa, how do you know?

I know this to be true because human behavior is very predictable. If a person consistently struggles with:

*Not feeling good enough
*Comparing themselves to others
*Wanting to always be the "best"
*Self-sabotage–creating unnecessary problems for themselves
*Engaging in negative self-talk when they make mistakes
*Staying in constant cycles of burn out

People who struggle with these things are most likely having a really hard time accepting and acknowledging their personal limitations/weaknesses. When we behave this way, it's a sign there may be an illusion that needs to be faced.

An illusion is a false idea or belief; a deceptive appearance or impression; or a thing that is wrongly perceived or interpreted. The false belief is that weaknesses make us weak and less valuable. As a result of this false belief, we are not able to allow ourselves to be who we really are or do what we are really capable of. By not embracing, recognizing, and accepting our limits, we actually behave in ways that bring harm to our Self. For example, I am a very empathetic, kind, and caring person. I listen well and have a way of communicating that helps people feel seen, known, and loved. These are some of my greatest strengths. Some people may assume that a person with these types of strengths is also very gentle. I used to think that about myself; that I was a gentle person. I really believed that I possessed that quality. I wanted to see myself as gentle and allow other people to experience that fruit in my life. Who wouldn't want that? Gentleness is such a lovely fruit of the spirit. But as I got to know myself better, I found out that I wasn't very gentle. Ouch!

Truth is, I am a very direct person who is extremely goal oriented. As a result, I tend to be a straight shooter in my communication. I am very gracious, smile a lot, love to laugh, and super encouraging. And I can sometimes be cross, abrupt, harsh, and inpatient. God's grace is sufficient enough for you to have both the fruits of the Spirit *and* limitations.

Earlier, I talked about how helpful it has been for me to receive feedback about my limitations from trusted people who work closely with me and know me well. In addition to the feedback I received, the Lord has helped me pay attention to the fruit of my behavior. In one particular season of work, I ended up having three clients abruptly end services with me within a two-month period. That was a highly unusual occurrence for me, as my clients tend to be very satisfied with my services and remain in treatment for the recommended length of time. This left me feeling unsettled, so naturally I started talking to God about how I was feeling. If you are not talking to Jesus and the Holy Spirit about what concerns you, you are missing out. The Holy Spirit reveals all things.

In my quiet time with Jesus, He showed me a pattern with myself. When I experienced intense resistance from my clients, I lost my capacity to be kind, gentle, and patient. In addition, I also noticed that all three clients were seen in the late evening, so the later the day got, the less patient I became. I realized that my problem in the situation was my crossness, impatience, and physically working too late into the evening. The Lord showed me my limitations; I was not gentle, I was impatient and I was not honoring my time and energy boundaries.

My initial response was to argue with God. I was like, "God, come on! I am a counselor, coach, and a Christian. There is no way I have a deficiency in this area." "Satan, I rebuke you! I have the fruit of the Spirit and the heart of the Father." I'm just gonna shame the devil and tell the truth, I was in denial. I was bound by an illusion. I believed that I was gentle, patient, and stewarding my energy well but that just wasn't true. I wrestled with God for a while because I didn't want to accept the truth about myself.

Sometimes we hold on to an illusion or false belief about ourselves because we are afraid. If I tell myself the truth about myself concerning my weakness, what does that say about me? Who am I? Will I still be valued and valuable? Will I be good enough? Will people still like me and still love me? Will I be able to accept myself?

Facing illusions is the place we can go to tell ourselves the truth about ourselves, other people, and our situation. Truth telling can be challenging, but it is also liberating. The bible says that *"we should know the truth and the truth will set us free"* (John 8:32). Let's lean into some biblical truth.

Confronting the Lies

So let's circle back. I mentioned some common statements and questions that can indicate someone has a religious mindset around self-acceptance. I want to address these illusions/mindsets with the word of God so you can receive God's permission to live in the reality of who you are and where you are.

Lie #1 – "God is perfect; therefore, I should strive for perfection. After all, the goal is to be like him."

Yes, in Matthew 5:48 the scripture reads, *"Be perfect for, I am perfect."* When God created the Earth and mankind, it was perfect and good in every way (Gen. 1). However, Adam and Eve's choices in the garden stripped us from God's original design for us to be perfect beings living in a pleasurable and perfect world.

"When sin came on the season our ability to reach perfection dissolved. A part of the reason Jesus came to Earth is to restore our places as children of God through the perfect blood sacrifice. By the blood of Jesus, all of our sins and faults are *covered*. Jesus' birth, death, and resurrection are all about restoring man to God and restoring the Earth through God's Kingdom. Remember, our restoration is a part of God's plan. "If we were perfect – or even capable of being perfect – there would have been no need for Jesus to save us. It is because of our imperfection that we receive everything God has to offer. (Agonkhese n.d.)"

God's promise is that we **will be** perfect when we see Him face to face, *"For when we see him, we shall be like him."* (1 John 3:2). Until then, we are living life between two gardens: The Garden of Eden and our Heavenly Home. On Earth, we are not called to the same level of perfection that God embodies. In the here and now, we are called to obedience, faithfulness, and growth. In the here and now, being "perfect" looks like obeying God's commands, remaining faithful to His word and will for your life, and staying engaged in discipleship (the process of following Jesus) so you can become *"fully mature not lacking any good thing."* (James 1:4).

#Lie #2. If I recognize my weakness in any way I am giving it power over me.

Recognizing your weakness does not give it power over you but ignoring it does. As we've stated repeatedly, *everyone* has weaknesses. Having limitations is normal for human beings. Not only is it normal, but God expects us to have weakness because we live in a broken and fallen world. The opposite of recognizing your weakness is ignoring it. If you intentionally ignore something that is a part of you, a part of who you are and how God made you, you are rejecting yourself. And we know what that leads to…low self-esteem and distorted identity. Not only are you rejecting yourself, but you are missing out on some key information to help you best navigate the life God has called you to.

People who ignore themselves are in denial of their limitation and often have a hard time:

*Asking for help
*Knowing what's appropriate to take on
*Choosing an educational path or career that is the best fit
*Wasting time and energy doing things they are not graced for
*Feeling like a failure or loser
*Loving and accepting themselves
*Extending grace to others

Accepting your weakness actually sets you free to be who you REALLY are; it frees you to be authentically you. While you stay engaged in obeying God and following Him, you also excuse yourself from having to be all things to all people in every situation. You free yourself from trying to be God and are positioned to experience acceptance as His son or daughter.

Recognizing and accepting your weakness empowers you to turn the right things over to Jesus. You can't give God anything you are not willing to first pick up. Invite Jesus into your weaknesses and allow Him to show you the things you need to see and understand. Let Him help you discover a path for your level up, break through, and healing. Because here's the thing, you don't know everything.

You did not create yourself. God created you. There may be some things in your life you see as weaknesses, but God placed them there to be tools. If it's a tool that fuels you into destiny and purpose, He may not remove it! What you see as a weakness is sometimes a strength or a shaping tool in the eyes of the one who created you, He would know.

For example, during a season of intense personal growth, I discovered that I was an enabler trapped in several codependent relationships. An enabler is someone who tends to support someone who is underfunctioning by doing for them what they need to do for themselves. Codependency is a dysfunctional relationship in which one person enables another person's addiction, poor mental health, irresponsibility, immaturity and/or under-achievement.

To be fair, I developed my enabling superpowers honestly. I am the daughter of an alcoholic and drug addict. Anyone who grows up in the home with at least one parent struggling with addiction or mental health issues watches someone prop the other person up. They watch someone hold this person together so they can function. The issue does not have to be addiction or poor mental health for codependency to exist, it was just the main culprit in my family situation.

All of those years spent watching someone take helping, fixing, serving, and giving too far left me with a framework for relationships rooted in the belief that when you really care for someone, it's your job to do everything you can to help them hold it together so you and the family can survive. The initial message I received is that it is okay to be unhealthy if you are trying to save someone you love.

This silent messaging became quite problematic for me. In my closest relationships, I often found myself giving my time, money, and energy far beyond my capacity. This cycle of service always left me feeling exhausted, unseen, and bitter. It wasn't until I recognized my behavior of enabling and reframed it as a weakness that I was able to find an effective pathway to healing and freedom. My entire life changed. God used my experience to help people process trauma and develop skills for overcoming codependent behaviors.

Now, I consider myself to be a recovering enabler. In my walk with Jesus, I have opened up to His healing power in many areas of weakness. But on this journey, sometimes seeing and sensing the heart of God concerning a struggling and broken person shatters my heart. Sometimes my heart crumbles under the weight of the situation, the depth of their pain, and the complexity of their twisted mindset.

In my personal life, I used to try to come from beneath that weight in my own strength. I would offer people more of my time, more of my attention, or even financial assistance. The more I gave in my own strength, the more deprecated and bitter I became. And oftentimes, the person remained stuck in their ways.

Once I stopped being overly responsible for other people, things changed. I felt the weight lift and began to lean into Jesus for heaven's solutions in their lives. Sometimes we would give just the right word for a person; provide the perfect example; soften their heart or mind; give them unusual strength to endure; or send them more help or support. Our efforts are nothing in comparison to one touch from the Father. When Jesus gets involved, everything changes.

I have come to discover that enabling behavior is not just a weakness, it's a tool that God uses to keep me in the process of becoming who He has called me to be. Yes, there are times when I am triggered to be overly helpful, giving, or fixing, but these days being triggered doesn't throw me back into a codependent cycle with someone. Instead, it empowers me to see more clearly God's heart for a person. This equips me to pray more fervently on their behalf, speak words of wisdom, knowledge, and understanding, and encourage them from the heart of the Father.

Most of all, I am triggered to declare boldly to God's people that He has the power to save, heal, deliver, and set free and if we stay in the process He provides us we will see His salvation and healing manifest in their lives. I know God uses this tool in my life to inspire others to believe Him, too.

Your weakness is a portal for God's glory. Don't despise it. Grow through it.

Lie #3 Accepting my weakness means I am giving into sin and not trying to be like Jesus.

When it comes to your identity, God wants you to be sober minded. Jesus encourages us not to think more highly of ourselves than we are (Rom. 12:3). There is a difference between accepting your weaknesses and deliberately walking in sin. We have all sinned and fallen short of the glory of God. Not Just Adam and Eve, Jezeblel and Ahab, but you and me. No one is without sin (Rom. 3:23) and any man who says that he is blameless is fooling himself (1 John 1:10).

We all have a predisposition to make mistakes and sometimes do things that are not pleasing to God. Weaknesses get a bad rep because they can be easily associated with sinful acts. For example, a person who is lustful may be more prone to having sex outside of marriage or cheating on their spouse. A person who is greedy may have a greater prosperity for stealing or cheating on their taxes. A person who is lazy may be more likely to let their home and property go without maintenance. I think it's logical to make these types of connections, but I don't think it is fair or useful.

Buying into the notion that people are bound and controlled by their weakness is erroneous. While strengths and weaknesses are a part of who we are, we have the power to choose how they manifest in our lives. We have the power to choose how we engage with them. Not only do we have our own willpower, most importantly we have access to the power of the Holy Spirit working inside of us. Check out these promises.

*God gives a way of escape. With every temptation, God provides a way of escape.

> "No temptation has overtaken you that is not common to man. God is faithful, and he will not let you be tempted beyond your ability, but with the temptation he will also provide the way of escape, that you may be able to endure it." (1 Cor. 10:13)

*You can do things God's way.

> "For God is working in you, giving you the desire and the power to do what pleases him." (Phil. 2:13)

*There is treasure inside of you.

> "But we have this treasure in jars of clay, to show that the surpassing power belongs to God and not to us." (2 Cor. 4:7)

*You can do it!

> "What appears humanly impossible is more than possible with God. For God can do what man cannot." (Luke 18:27)

That's why knowing as much as you can about yourself; the good, the bad, and the ugly, is critical. Knowledge is power. When you see yourself for who you really are, you can make empowered and informed decisions for your life. Who doesn't want that????

How to Embrace Your Weaknesses

Let's talk about a couple of strategies for embracing your limitations. These free tools are particularly helpful in managing your thoughts and behavior on a daily basis.

Manage Your Self-Talk.

Self-talk is your internal dialogue. It's influenced by your subconscious mind and it reveals your thoughts, beliefs, questions, and ideas. "Self-talk can be both negative and positive. It can be encouraging, and it can be distressing. Your thoughts are the source of your emotions and mood. The conversations you have with yourself can be destructive or beneficial. They influence how you feel about yourself and how you respond to events in your life. (Holland 2020)"

Self-talk is something you do naturally throughout your waking hours. Self-talk is an involuntary reflex of the brain like breathing is to the lungs. Many people move around throughout their day entertaining negative beliefs, questions, and ideas. People who have a lot of negative self-talk are typically unhappy, frustrated, and discontented concerning themselves and their lives. Some folks don't actually have major problems in their lives, but they maintain a baseline of sadness and discontent.

In my work, negative feelings about yourself, others, or your situation can ALWAYS, and I do mean ALWAYS be traced back to negative self-talk. A negative internal dialogue includes thoughts, beliefs, questions, and ideas like:

"I can't get anything right."

"Look, I am screwing up something else."
"I don't think I fit in."
"I don't belong here."
"I am so stupid."
"If I wasn't so fat, maybe I wouldn't be single."
"If I don't do this, it won't get done."
"If I want something done right, I must take care of it myself."

Reflection

Take a moment to think about your self-talk. What are some of the negative things you think or say to yourself? Write them in the space below.

Many of us subconsciously entertain this type of negativity all day long. No wonder we struggle with poor self-esteem! How could we not? The key to flipping the switch is to begin managing your inner dialogue instead of allowing it to run wild and control you. The simplest way to combat this is by using positive self-talk. A positive inner dialogue says things like:

"Everyone makes mistakes. It's ok."

"I learned something new. I will do better next time."

"I am learning -–not failing."

"It takes time to make connections with people. I can be patient."

"I have the right + responsibility to be wherever God sends me."

"I love and respect my body. Anyone I date will have feel that way about it too."

"I am on a team, all the balls are not in my court."

"I am worthy of love and respect."

If you need help changing your self-talk, see the ***Self-Talk Swap*** activity in the appendix section near the back of the book.

Ask God for help. Embracing our limitations can be a difficult task. All of the messages we receive about our value being rooted in our accomplishments can be hard to silence. When I encourage people to embrace their limitations, I am often met with resistance. Why? Because admitting that you have limits can be humbling. It's a call to swallow your pride. It's an invitation to wrestle with your identity. For many, admitting to their limitations causes deep feelings of guilt and shame to arise. Guilt says I've done something wrong. This is a lie. You are a flawed human, that's how humanity works. You don't have limitations because you've done something wrong, you have limitations because you are alive.

Shame says that I am wrong. This is a lie. God has chosen you; He knows you, sees you and loves you. His word declares that you are the **right**eousness of Christ (2 Cor. 5:21), which is the complete opposite of being wrong. Because of what Christ has done, you are made **right**. God said it and that settles it.

If you resonate with these deeply embedded feelings of guilt and shame, it's time to ask God for help. I am not talking about a cute little one-time prayer for God's help, I am talking about contending for freedom in your heart and mind. I am talking about crying out to God to meet you where you are right now. I am talking about meditating on the scripture so that the truth of His word can take root in your soul and come fully alive in your life. It's time to contend for your healing.

> *"I sought the LORD, and he answered me; he delivered me from all my fears."* (Ps. 34:4)

> *"In my distress I called upon the Lord, and cried unto my God: he heard my voice out of his temple, and my cry came before him, even into his ears."* (Ps. 18:6)

> *"Let your roots grow down into him, and let your lives be built on him. Then your faith will grow strong in the truth you were taught, and you will overflow with thankfulness."* (Col. 2:7)

> *"Behold, I will bring to it health and healing, and I will heal them and reveal to them abundance of prosperity and security."* (Jer. 33:6)

Lean Into God's Strength

One of the major strategies for breakthrough in any area of our lives is to lean into God's strength. When it comes to breaking out of a mental stronghold that you've been in, possibly since early childhood, you need God's power! Our God is strong and mighty (Ps. 147:5). He can do anything (Luke 1:37). There is nothing too hard for the Lord (Jer. 37:32). With God, all things are possible (Mark 9:23). God's word is true, but you can only access His strength by leaning into it.

To lean in, you cause something to rest against. To lean in, you rely on or derive support from someone or something. Let's allow our hearts and minds to take rest in the truth of God's word. Do you rely on Jesus? Do you count on the Holy Spirit? Leaning into His strength is a call to trust.

It's easy to trust someone that you know well and share a deep level of intimacy with. Sometimes we are unable to access God's strength because we don't know Him well enough to trust Him. I am not making this statement to judge you and suggest that you have no trust in God. I am simply suggesting that it may be time for you to increase your capacity to trust Him in this season of your life. Our relationship with Jesus is not one in which we "arrive." There is no coming to a place in this life where we know all there is to know of Him, his character, and His ways. We will learn to trust Him more and more until we see Him face to face. Perhaps this is one of your growth moments.

> *"Blessed is the man who trusts in the Lord, whose trust is the Lord. He is like a tree planted by water, that sends out its roots by the stream, and does not fear when heat comes, for its leaves remain green, and is*

not anxious in the year of drought, for it does not cease to bear fruit." (Jer. 17:7-8)

"And those who know your name put their trust in you, for you, O Lord, have not forsaken those who seek you." (Ps. 9:10)

"When I am afraid, I put my trust in you." (Ps. 5:6)

"You keep him in perfect peace whose mind is stayed on you, because he trusts in you." (Isa. 26:3)

Not only does God want you to rely on Him, He wants to support you. He wants to bear the mental, emotional, and spiritual weight of this situation. God wants to hold you up. God longs to assist you. His will is to enable you to function. Listen to what He says:

"Behold, God is my helper; the Lord is the upholder of my life." (Ps. 54:4)

"Fear not, for I am with you; be not dismayed, for I am your God; I will strengthen you, I will help you, I will uphold you with my righteous right hand." (Isaiah 41:10)

"And my God will supply every need of yours according to his riches in glory in Christ Jesus." (Phil. 4:19)

"But they who wait for the Lord shall renew their strength; they shall mount up with wings like eagles; they shall run and not be weary; they shall walk and not faint." (Isa. 40:31)

Will you **receive** God's support and lean into His strength in your process?

Expect To Make Mistakes

One of the major ways to receive healing and freedom in the area of self-esteem is to expect yourself to make mistakes. Expect to not always win. Expect to not come out on top every time. Don't get me wrong, we need to be hopeful, positive, and expect the good, but failure to accept that things will not always go the way you want them to, is immature and unrealistic. We must increase our capacity to navigate this life knowing that God is for us, and in the end we win. We must accept that we are in a broken and fallen world.

The better we get at accepting both of those realities, the healthier and happier we will be. Remember, God made you just the way you are. He loves you. He loves you and has plans to strengthen and level you up. Receive His unconditional love and intentionally offer some love and acceptance to yourself.

Practice Self-Compassion

How do you treat others when you see them struggling? Let's say you've been working really hard for the past six months and it's time to take a break. You've booked a week-long beach trip to reward yourself and just unwind. and you'd like to take a friend along who could make great company. So, you invite the friend to join you and they are free on those dates, but there's just one problem.

Your friend says to you, "Thanks so much for the invite, I am free but not sure if I can make it. To be honest, I've been feeling super self-conscious about the 25lbs I've gained this year. The thought of being at the beach and looking flabby kind of stresses me out."

How would you respond?

A. "I understand. If I had packed on so many pounds, I probably wouldn't be going either, Thanks for considering."

B. "How did you get so big, bruh?"

C. "Friend, you are amazing from the inside out. It's been a tough year. I have faith in your ability to get your weight under control, but you are still allowed to be happy and enjoy your life in the process."

Hopefully you selected "C". If you chose A or B, you may not have friends for very long!

When it comes to other people, the bible admonishes us to be kind, gentle, encouraging, and to be helpful and supportive (Eph. 4:32, 1 Cor. 14:4-7). If God calls you to treat others with that type of compassion, what makes you think that He doesn't expect you to treat yourself that way? God even promises to treat you with compassion. Lamentations 3:22 says, *"Because of the LORD's great love we are not consumed, for his compassions never fail. They are new every morning; great is your faithfulness!"* If you are following Jesus and His teaching, self-compassion should be a major component of your feelings, thoughts, and behaviors.

Not only that, but Jesus commands us to love others as we love ourselves (Matt. 22:39). This commandment is a call to love others well out of the love and care you show yourself. This sounds like a call to self-love and compassion. Simply put, self-compassion is offering yourself the same type of kindness, gentleness, and acceptance you offer to others. Self-compassion is a practice that I use in all of my work. It was developed by Dr. Kristin Neff, an Educational Psychologist and researcher. Self-compassion has three elements: 1. self-kindness vs. self-judgment; 2. common humanity vs isolation; and 3. mindfulness vs. over-identification. Self-compassion is not self-pity, self-indulgence, or self-esteem. To learn more about self-compassion, visit www.thehealingpros.com/selfcompassion and download a free resource.

CHAPTER 6

Valuing Others

The final component of Healthy Self-Esteem is valuing others. It's pretty easy to see how valuing yourself is critical to having a healthy self – but valuing others? How does that fit into the equation?

When you meet someone new, how do you know whether or not you will like them? Is it "like" at first sight? Or does it take you more time to figure it out? What are the green flags for knowing that someone would make a great friend/acquaintance for you?

We all have our things. For me, I tend to connect with people who are naturally curious about me as a person, not just what I do for a living. Why? This communicates they might value people for who they are, not just what they do. I love meeting people who were born in the same year as me or within a year or two. It's really fun to have the same cultural references, especially if they are into 90's R&B!!! Why? This could mean they understand my worldview.

I adore meeting people who are obsessed with organization and interior design. Basically, women who overdose on HGTV. Why? I value hospitality and this may be a cue that they appreciate fun, beautiful, and peaceful spaces for themselves and the people they love.

I also get excited when I meet someone and learn that we watch the same TV shows, like Gilmore Girls, Crazy Ex-Girlfriend, Jane

The Virgin, or On My Block. Why? This tells me they may share a similar sense of humor, or fascination with and love for all things relationship.

Generally speaking, people who like themselves like people who are like them. Let's face it, we like people who are like us. And we tend to value people that we like. Liking yourself is beneficial to you and for others. If you don't like and accept yourself, it's hard to value yourself. If you don't value yourself, valuing others is not as easy as one might think.

The world teaches us to value:

> People who have similar strengths.
> People who are accomplished.
> People who are strong.
> People who are beautiful.
> People who have money.
> People who are popular.
> People who are extroverted.
> People who are talented.
> People who are influencers.
> People who have power.

So what happens when we meet people we don't like? What about the people you don't enjoy being around? What is it about them that gets under your skin?

For me, I find myself feeling annoyed with people who are timid or if they have a hard time speaking up or asking for what they want. I struggle with people who appear to be open and easy going, but their behavior suggests the opposite. They are actually quite controlling. I sometimes get frustrated with people who can't express how they feel about something or constantly say they don't know how they feel. I also tend to move away from people who look dirty or don't smell good. I feel very uncomfortable in their presence.

When we notice ourselves not liking someone or feeling bothered or annoyed by them, we should train ourselves to become curious by asking ourselves, what is it about this person that is unnerving to me?

1. *We despise in others what we despise in ourselves.*

Oftentimes, a person can serve as a mirror to us. You don't have to be able to see what you hate in yourself in order for it to unnerve you. In this case, we are unable to see how our experience with this person is parallel to our true selves; good, bad, or indifferent. Identifying what about this person unnerves you can help you become more self-aware. For example, I am easily annoyed by timid people because I used to be one of them.

In my life, timidity was a symptom of excessive people pleasing. I used to be afraid to speak up for fear that I would offend someone or just be disliked for standing out in the crowd. I found my voice in high school and college but started silencing myself again once I started my career. It took me a couple of years to experience freedom in that area again and it was a difficult process for me as a highly educated black female in predominantly white male spaces. When I meet people who are timid, I am subconsciously yelling, "Speak up and be your authentic self, sis." "Bro, can you please allow yourself to take up space in this room. You are worthy! Act like it."

When I see timidity in others during interactions, I see my former self and go into a bit of self-protective mode. We ain't going back there! If this resonates with you, I am right there with you and it's important to increase our ability to show people grace. While you may have similar experiences with others, we are all different people with diverse callings and processes. The same way God is working in you, he is working in others, too.

We can choose to be patient with ourselves and others because God is patient. We can choose to still hold this person and ourselves in high regard, even if they do get on our last nerve! Just like you, they are created in the image of almighty God. Just like you, they are worthy to be treated with dignity, love, and respect, even if you don't enjoy their God design.

2. **We value personal attributes or characteristics more than we value people.**

Ouch. It really hurt to write that last sentence. It stings but it's true. As Christians we often take on the world's beliefs and behaviors for navigating our relationships. Valuing strengths and qualities is rooted in the perfectionist mindset. If people can possess good qualities, then they can be worthy or valuable. Once again, that is not what God says. His word tells us that if you want to see the greatest of these, look at the least of these (Matt.23:11) In the Kingdom of God, we are called to visit people who are in prisons (sinners), children who have been abandoned by their parents (delinquents), and women who have lost their status in society or facing poverty (widows) (James 1:27). God tells us that the last shall be first and the first shall be last (Matt. 19:30).

No matter how much people irritate or annoy us due to their bad habits, poor choices, weaknesses, or character flaws, as God's people we need to make sure that we value people, period. All people. Why? Because all people are created in the image of the almighty God. We are not called to just honor Christians, successful people, wealthy people, or powerful people. We are called to honor and value all people. You cannot have healthy self-esteem without valuing others. Some of the healthiest people are people who value **ALL** people. Loving all people is a deep revelation of the nature and character of Jesus Christ.

When I say honor, love, and value all people, I do mean all people.

Black and brown people.
LGBQT+ people.
Women.
Children.
Elderly people.
Physically and Mentally Impaired people.
Non-Christian people.
White people.
Mean people.
Lazy people.
Hateful people.
Broken people.
Single people.
Lost people.
Homeless people.
All people.

God loves and values you so much that He sent Jesus to die for you! Guess what? He sent Jesus to die for all people. He didn't die for personal qualities and strengths. He died for people. Want to be like Jesus? Learn to value what He values. Value People.

3. ***We devalue people because we feel jealous.***

Jealousy is a feeling or an act of showing envy toward someone or their achievements and advantages. Jealousy can look like fierce protection or vigilance of one's rights or possessions.

Envy is a feeling of discontented or resentful longing aroused by someone else's possessions, qualities, or luck. When we are envious, we want what someone else has.

Any time that feelings of jealousy or envy show up on the scene, we automatically know that in the moment we are struggling with the first component of Healthy self-esteem, valuing ourselves. We know this because when we hold value for ourselves, we are committed to the belief that we are good enough, worthy, and content with ourselves despite what is happening in someone else's life. Why? Because we are fully committed to the belief that our value is innate and God-given. It does not shift based on what we or others say or do.

If we notice someone else's achievement, advantage, strengths, or possessions and become **discontent** or **resentful**, that is a sign that we are devaluing them as a person. If we truly value others and God's plan for them, our hearts and minds can celebrate them shining, growing, and increasing without feeling less than, left out, or left behind. If we find ourselves feeling discontent or resentful when others succeed, we need to check our belief systems about ourselves *and* about our God. It is the Father's good pleasure to give gifts to His children (Luke 12:32). The Lord rains on both the just and the unjust (Matt. 5:45). God is faithful. He will do it. (1 Thess. 5:24). Feelings of jealousy or envy are evidence that we are entertaining thoughts or ideas that do not align with the truth of God's word.

What lies are you believing?

"I can never lose weight."
"No one will ever want me."
"God doesn't really love me."
"God has forgotten me."
"If I don't get _____, I will never be happy."
"Once I _____, I will be happy."

These are not truths–they are lies. Lies that are destroying your self-image and distorting your ability to value yourself. Lies that are most likely hurting the intimacy in your relationships and maybe some of the deeper connections you long for are blocked by your jealous and envious thoughts, feelings, or behavior. Healthy people can sense jealousy and envy and will back away. I certainly back away when I detect it in relationships. Why?

Because you cannot trust someone who is jealous or envious. They are not emotionally safe with themselves because they aren't fully connected to their value. If they are not safe with themselves, how can you truly feel safe with them? It doesn't mean you can't be friends, but it often warrants a decrease in intimacy, as jealous and envious people are prone to sabotaging relationships with themselves and others.

The Truth About Valuing Others

1. **You don't have to agree with someone to value them.**

We all have our own morals, values, and beliefs. Jesus' commandment to love others is not limited to people who share your convictions. If you struggle to accept and value people who are different from you, you are most likely wrestling with a spirit of control. Remember, you are not God. Other people have the right to believe, think, feel, and behave as they see fit. As a non-deity, your job is to love and value them. God's job is to judge. Release the need to have everything align with your ways now, in Jesus' name. Just like God will judge you, He will judge others. If you want to be judged harshly by God, continue trying to control others through your judgment (Matt. 7:2). If you want to receive mercy, both now and later, show mercy. Release control and stop carrying a false responsibility to control others.

2. **You don't have to accept someone's beliefs or behaviors to value them.**

Once again, all people are created by God with innate worth and value. A person's value does not fluctuate. Value does not shift over time. God loves us with an everlasting love. Even when people believe something sick or twisted, God still sees them as valuable. Even when people behave in horrible and unGodly ways, God still values them. Have you ever held thoughts or beliefs that you are now ashamed of? Have you ever done anything that could send you to hell in a handbasket? Of course you have! For *all* have sinned and fallen short of the glory of God (Rom. 3:23).

You may not think that way or do those things anymore, but that does not make you perfect. You are still in process. Because of this, we need to be careful about judging others because of their thoughts or actions. The bible says that we should take heed lest we fall (1 Cor. 10:12). Instead of judging them, we can opt to speak truth in love and pray for them.

The same God that broke the chains off of your mind, brought you out of fornication and sexual perversion, and taught you how to stop lying is the Lord of all! If He did that for you, what makes you think He can't do that for someone else? He is no respecter of person (Acts 10:34). If you think you should wait to value another until their behavior is acceptable to you, put away your pride! Pride comes before the fall (Prov. 16:18). God gives strength to the weak and He resists the proud (James 4:6). I bind the spirit of pride now, in Jesus' name. We break every deception and lie that has kept you from valuing others properly. When we devalue people, we make them our enemies. Making someone your enemy is a choice.

Where would you be if God devalued you for your beliefs and behaviors? Where would you be if God decided that you were not worthy of healing, deliverance, or freedom until you could find the power to straighten yourself out?

We don't have that power; He has the power. Jesus has power over all. What might be possible in your life and those around you if you made the choice to value people the way Jesus values them? Let me tell you what would happen. This world would be turned upside down and inside out with the saving, healing, and delivering power of Jesus! We would begin to experience more modern-day miracles, families would be restored, sickness healed, and minds would be mended.

The power of the cross is Love. When we start loving all people without hesitation, more of God's glory will consume the Earth. Being offended by people's differences is the bait of Satan. So many of us reject people because we believe that rejecting them is a mark of purity and commitment to God. It's quite the opposite. Jesus loved and valued people who were drastically different from him and it shifted the culture in that day so much that millions of people still follow his teachings today. Stop letting the devil trick you and steal your God given authority in this Earth.

w3. **You can value someone you no longer want in your life.**

Some relationships have an expiration date for a variety of reasons. People relocate. People cheat. People betray us. People ghost us. People outgrow us and we can outgrow them. God shifts us. Relationships end. No matter the reason, valuing someone is a choice. You don't have to be in a relationship with anyone to value them as a person. No matter what someone has done (or hasn't done), holding them in a place of value honors God and honors your own heart. You just have to find a way to value them that is <u>consistent</u> with the reality of the situation and is appropriate for your emotional ability and capacity.

4. **You can value people who have hurt you.**

Yes, I said what I said. You can value people who hurt you. No one is perfect. People make mistakes. Sometimes they take responsibility and sometimes they don't. However, anyone you cannot value, you release your peace and power to. An inability to value someone who has hurt you is an indicator that you have not (or need to continue) the oh so challenging work of forgiving those who have hurt you. Be kind and compassionate to one another, forgiving each other, just as Christ God forgave you (Eph. 4:32). People who have hurt us are often enemies, until we forgive them. God calls us to bless those who curse (hurt) us and despitefully use us (Luke 6:28). If you don't forgive others, your prayers will be hindered (Mark 11:25).

I am not suggesting that you exhort or encourage someone who has manipulated, controlled, or abused you. It may not be wise to create space or lean into a relationship that needs to end for a good reason. What I am saying is that working through the hurt and releasing forgiveness will set your heart free from the emotional, spiritual, physical, and intellectual toll that bitterness takes on us.

The narrative of bitter people is that of the victim. A person bound by a spirit of bitterness/unforgiveness sees themselves as powerless, assaulted, defenseless, and weak. This type of narrative is an enemy to healthy self-esteem. People who are hurt by others are sometimes secretly blaming and shaming themselves for the role they played in the misfortune. You may be trying to figure out what's stopping you from going back to school, starting that business, or pursuing that new hobby. Oftentimes our inability to move forward is the fruit of bitterness and unforgiveness. Bitterness takes a toll on your healthy self. I once heard someone say that unforgiveness is a portal of demonic activity in your life. When I heard those words, I felt it in every fiber of my being. I could instantly connect where bitterness/unforgiveness/devaluing others was causing me to bring more damage to myself.

If this resonates with you, I want you to place your hands on your head and your heart and speak this over yourself:

"Father, I forgive _____ for hurting me. I understand that forgiveness is a decision and not a feeling. Today, I choose to walk in obedience with your command to forgive so that I can have peace, healing, and forgiveness. I trust you with my process. I trust that you will lead me to a pathway of recovering from this that is just right for me. I commit to walking this out with you now in Jesus' name. Amen!"

5. **Learning how to value others can help you better value yourself.**

What comes first, the chicken or the egg? I think the logical pathway for learning self-love, acceptance, and value is to start off by cultivating it inside of yourself with the help of the Holy Spirit and allowing it to flow out onto others. But as you know, God works in mysterious ways. When it comes to our healing and breakthrough, He uses what He wants, when He wants, How he wants.

We don't always get a say in how our healing manifests and breaks out. God can use anyone and anything, which means the pathway to learning to better value, love, and accept yourself could break out when you press into offering acceptance to others. Even if valuing others isn't your strong suit, if God is leading and guiding you in that direction with others, trust His leading. If the power of Jesus is involved, whatever He does *through* you can cause transformation and healing to work *in* you! Whatever Jesus does in you; He can release into the lives of others through you. So I don't know about you, but I don't care if He does it in me or through me first, just give me my healing! I want to be free.

6. **Valuing Others Brings Freedom**

When you can truly value all people regardless of your history with them, their beliefs and behaviors, their sexual orientation, gender, skin color, political affiliation, denomination, age, ability, etc, you bear the mark of a healed and healthy person. You are free from offense and free from guilt & shame. You don't have to look down on others in order to feel good about yourself. The enemy can no longer control your thoughts and feelings. When this happens you are healed. It doesn't mean that your life is perfect. It means that every relationship is functionally optimally and everything is just so.

It just means you can hold value for yourself and others even in imperfection. It means you have been healed and you are now positioned to pass on and share that healing with everyone and everything connected to you.

CHAPTER 7

The Journey Ahead

Wow! I can't believe we've reached the end of this book. While this chapter marks the end of the reading, your journey will continue. So here's the big question. How do we take what we've learned in these pages and continue to apply it to our daily lives?

We continue our growth by choosing a specific area of our relationship with Self to focus on and choose an intentional way to keep growing in that area. Take a look at the four major areas of self-esteem below. I have included some affirmations in each category. Place a check mark beside each item that you find to be true for you. Don't overthink it. Just be honest and keep working through the list.

Valuing Myself

- I pay attention to my own needs.
- I allow myself to rest.
- I can relax when I need to do so.
- I can take time off to recuperate.
- I use my time to invest in myself.
- I use my money to invest in myself.
- I am valuable.
- I love myself.

- I am worthy to receive love.
- No matter what happens in me, to me, or around me, my value never changes.

Total _____

Acknowledging & Accepting My Strengths

- I know what my strengths are and feel good about them.
- I can accept a compliment.
- I can say yes to opportunities to advance.
- I feel confident in my ability to do what I am good at.
- I am good at several things.
- I can accept others celebrating my gifts or talents.
- I can share my gifts, skills, and talents with others.
- I don't hide my strengths to fit in with others.

Total _____

Acknowledging & Accepting My Weaknesses

- I am able to articulate my limitations and weaknesses.
- I know that I am not perfect and I'm okay with that.
- I am not striving to get everything right all the time.
- I do not need to overcome all of my weaknesses to be a better person.
- It is ok for me to make mistakes.
- Making mistakes does not make me a failure.
- I am worthy, even when I make mistakes.
- I do not compare myself to others.

- If I start comparing myself to others, I can recognize it and stop.

Total _____

Valuing Others

- I don't have to put others down to feel good about myself.
- I can provide compliments to others on their strengths.
- I value people as God's children, even if they are not my preference.
- I respect others, even if they do not respect me.
- I treat all people with dignity and respect, regardless of their worldview.
- I see the value of all people, even if they are from a different background.
- I hold value for people even if we have different religious backgrounds or beliefs.

Total _____

Look at the four areas above. Add up the number of checks in each category. The category with the lowest score is most likely your growth area for improving your Self-Esteem.

Notice the areas where you struggled most to identify with the statements. Ask the Lord which areas He would like for you to focus on as you continue your journey. Take 2-3 minutes to sit quietly and allow the Holy Spirit to highlight an area of focus for you.

What area will you choose to focus on as you continue your journey? Check one below.

- Valuing Yourself
- Embracing Your Strengths
- Embracing Your Limitations
- Valuing Others

Now that you've identified an area of focus, it's time to set a goal.

SMART Goals

I believe in setting SMART Goals. SMART is an acronym that stands for setting goals that are specific, measurable, realistic, and time specific. See the graph below for a quick overview of SMART goals.
("SMART Goals Template" n.d.)

Now that we understand how to set a goal, let's use a Goal Detail sheet.
Here is an example of a Goal Detail. Read this example. You will write your own goal statement in the next step.

Sample Goal Detail

Goal Statement. Write your goal here.

I will increase my self-esteem by improving my ability to value myself over the next six months.

Key Motivations. Write, then rank, your key motivations.
   -Feeling better about myself improves my confidence.
   -I really want to see myself the way that God sees me.
   -I am sick of feeling run down and tired all the time.

Next Steps. List the first few projects or tasks that make up your goal.
   -Book myself for a monthly mani-pedi.
   -Submit a time off request for one week in August.
   -Post some affirmations on my mirror and start saying them aloud every during my morning and evening routines.

Evaluate. Decide how you'll know when you are doing better.
   -I will know that I am doing better when I feel less resentful about my work and I am able to acknowledge my own success.

Celebration. Decide how you'll celebrate your success.
   -When I reach this goal, I will celebrate by purchasing myself a bracelet that reminds me of my value.

Create your goal on the blank goal detail page in the Appendix.

This goal setting exercise is something you can use for any area of your life, not just around improving your relationship with Self. I encourage you to find other ways to use this format to help you move forward with purpose and intention.

There is one very important thing that I haven't mentioned. This journey of building healthy self-esteem is a lifelong journey. It didn't start with this book and it won't end here. Building healthy self-esteem is a process of **rediscovering** ourselves over and over again. If we are truly following Jesus, we'll be growing and changing until we meet him face to face.

The beauty of it all is that you are not alone. I am just one of many people who dedicate their lives to helping people live with intention and purpose. I am so glad that God saw fit to connect us through this book.

I am so proud of you for taking this journey with me. More importantly, I hope that you are just as proud of yourself. I pray that our time together has encouraged you to know that it's okay for you to be exactly where you are. You are in a learning and growing process called Life. God is for you, and He is with you. He did not make any mistakes by creating you the way you are. If there are things about you that need to change, His grace is sufficient. All you have to do is confess what needs to be confessed and do your part through faith and work. That's your part. The rest is up to God and His perfect timing.

Keep trusting God in your process.
Keep moving forward.

APPENDIX

Scriptures for Embracing My Weaknesses

Embracing biblical truth will help you embrace, accept and love yourself, despite our weaknesses. Read the scriptures below. Put a mark or check beside the ones that resonate with you most. Use the tips in this book to begin incorporating the scriptures you choose into your daily life.

> "But he said to me, 'My grace is sufficient for you, for my power is made perfect in weakness.' Therefore I will boast all the more gladly about my weaknesses, so that Christ's power may rest on me." -2 Corinthians 12:9-10

> "I can do all this through him who gives me strength." -Philippians 4:13

> "The Lord is close to the brokenhearted and saves those who are crushed in spirit." -Psalm 34:18

> "So do not fear, for I am with you; do not be dismayed, for I am your God. I will strengthen you and help you; I will uphold you with my righteous right hand." -Isaiah 41:10

"In the same way, the Spirit helps us in our weakness. We do not know what we ought to pray for, but the Spirit himself intercedes for us through wordless groans." -Romans 8:26

"I praise you because I am fearfully and wonderfully made; your works are wonderful, I know that full well." -Psalm 139:14

"Come to me, all you who are weary and burdened, and I will give you rest."—Matthew 11:28-30

"Trust in the Lord with all your heart and lean not on your own understanding; in all your ways submit to him, and he will make your paths straight." -Proverbs 3:5-6

"Cast all your anxiety on him because he cares for you." -1 Peter 5:7 (NIV)

"My sacrifice, O God, is a broken spirit; a broken and contrite heart you, God, will not despise." -Psalm 51:17

"For I know the plans I have for you, declares the Lord, plans to prosper you and not to harm you, plans to give you hope and a future." -Jeremiah 29:11

"Not only so, but we also glory in our sufferings, because we know that suffering produces perseverance; perseverance, character; and character, hope." -Romans 5:3-4

"My flesh and my heart may fail, but God is the strength of my heart and my portion forever." -Psalm 73:26

Scriptures for Embracing My Weaknesses

"For the Spirit God gave us does not make us timid, but gives us power, love, and self-discipline." -2 Timothy 1:7

"Cast your cares on the Lord and he will sustain you; he will never let the righteous be shaken." -Psalm 55:22

"Let us then approach God's throne of grace with confidence, so that we may receive mercy and find grace to help us in our time of need." -Hebrews 4:16

"But those who hope in the Lord will renew their strength. They will soar on wings like eagles; they will run and not grow weary, they will walk and not faint." -Isaiah 40:31

"Therefore we do not lose heart. Though outwardly we are wasting away, yet inwardly we are being renewed day by day." -2 Corinthians 4:16-18

"God is our refuge and strength, an ever-present help in trouble." -Psalm 46:1

"May the God of hope fill you with all joy and peace as you trust in him, so that you may overflow with hope by the power of the Holy Spirit." -Romans 15:13

Self-Talk Swap Activity

NOTE: This is a two-day activity.

DAY 1

Step 1: Spend one day examining your self-talk, take notice of any negative ideas, questions, attitudes, beliefs, or statements that show up in your thinking. Write them down somewhere for one whole day.

Step 2: Once you have your negative self-talk list, enter them inside in the table below.

NEGATIVE SELF-TALK

DAY 2

Note: The rest of this activity will take 45-60 Minutes.

Step 3: Read Philippians 4:6-9 to yourself aloud four times. Pause for 2-3 minutes in between the readings and listen to God. This step takes a little time, but God's word has the power to unlock new things and good things in every part of you. Take about 15 minutes to walk through this step. You are worth the time.

Reading #1

Action: Listen for a word or phrase God is highlighting in this passage for you.

> ⁶ Do not be anxious about anything, but in every situation, by prayer and petition, with thanksgiving, present your requests to God. ⁷ And the peace of God, which transcends all understanding, will guard your hearts and your minds in Christ Jesus.
>
> ⁸ Finally, brothers and sisters, whatever is true, whatever is noble, whatever is right, whatever is pure, whatever is lovely, whatever is admirable—if anything is excellent or praiseworthy—think about such things. ⁹ Whatever you have learned or received or heard from me, or seen in me— put it into practice. And the God of peace will be with you.

Action: What word or phrase did God highlight for you in this passage? Write it below.

Reading #2

Read the passage aloud again. This time, aim to see yourself or your life in the passage.

> ⁶ Do not be anxious about anything, but in every situation, by prayer and petition, with thanksgiving, present your

Self-Talk Swap Activity

requests to God. [7] And the peace of God, which transcends all understanding, will guard your hearts and your minds in Christ Jesus.

[8] Finally, brothers and sisters, whatever is true, whatever is noble, whatever is right, whatever is pure, whatever is lovely, whatever is admirable—if anything is excellent or praiseworthy—think about such things. [9] Whatever you have learned or received or heard from me, or seen in me— put it into practice. And the God of peace will be with you.

Action: Tell God how this connects to your life right now. Write your thoughts and feelings below.

Reading #3

Action: Read the passage aloud once again. When you are finished, close your eyes and be quiet. Allow God to speak to you.

[6] Do not be anxious about anything, but in every situation, by prayer and petition, with thanksgiving, present your requests to God. [7] And the peace of God, which transcends all understanding, will guard your hearts and your minds in Christ Jesus.

[8] Finally, brothers and sisters, whatever is true, whatever is noble, whatever is right, whatever is pure, whatever is lovely, whatever is admirable—if anything is excellent or praiseworthy—think about such things. [9] Whatever you have learned or received or heard from me, or seen in me— put it into practice. And the God of peace will be with you.

Action: Close your eyes. Be still and quiet for 2-3 minutes. Allow God to speak to you.

Reading #4

Action: Read the passage aloud again.

> ⁶ Do not be anxious about anything, but in every situation, by prayer and petition, with thanksgiving, present your requests to God. ⁷ And the peace of God, which transcends all understanding, will guard your hearts and your minds in Christ Jesus.
>
> ⁸ Finally, brothers and sisters, whatever is true, whatever is noble, whatever is right, whatever is pure, whatever is lovely, whatever is admirable—if anything is excellent or praiseworthy—think about such things. ⁹ Whatever you have learned or received or heard from me, or seen in me—put it into practice. And the God of peace will be with you.

Action: God has spoken to you. Write your response to God in the space below.

Step 4: With the Holy Spirit's help, create a positive thought/statement to serve as a replacement of your negative self-talk identified in Step 2. Maybe even be a scripture.

Self-Talk Swap Activity

NEGATIVE SELF-TALK	NEW SELF-TALK

Step 5: Get this new, God-inspired positive self-talk in your spirit! You can do this by engaging with your new thoughts in the following ways:

*Post your new thoughts on your bathroom mirror. This will position you to read them at the beginning and end each day (if you practice proper hygiene).

*Write your new self-talk on index cards and keep them inside your backpack or purse to engage with them throughout your day. Look at yourself in the mirror each day and say your statements aloud.

*Record yourself reading the statements and listen to yourself speak to yourself. This is a great alternative to looking in the mirror.

*Type your list on a note inside your phone.

*Use a program like Canva to create an inspiring design for your statements. Save the photos in your phone.

*Create a positive self-talk folder in your photos or on Pinterest.

Step 6: Engage with your new thoughts daily. Old thinking habits die hard. The brain is a bit lazy. If you have been engaging in a particular way of thinking for a long period of time, your brain is very comfortable with those thoughts. They are a familiar pattern;

a rhythm. One of the best ways to break that up is to expose your brain intentionally and consistently to new information. The more you "think" positively, the more open your brain and your spirit will become to believing, committing to, and receiving the new thought pattern. Even if it seems silly, do it. Build intentional positive self-talk into your life as a discipline. Eventually it will become natural and your WHOLE life will change.

Self-Esteem SMART Goal Worksheet

Goal Statement. Write your goal here.

Key Motivations. Write, then rank, your key motivations.
-
-
-

Next Steps. List the first few projects or tasks that make up your goal.
-
-
-

Timeline

I commit to intentionally focus on this area of my self-esteem.

I will begin working on this goal on the following date _____.

I will maintain this focus for _____ months.

Evaluate. Decide how you'll know when you are doing better.

Celebration. Decide how you'll celebrate your success.

References

Agonkhese, Sophie. "50 Effective Goals to Set for Yourself This Year." My Cup Runs Over. Accessed December 5, 2023. https://mycuprunsover.ca/goals-to-set-for-yourself.

Amodeo, John. What It Really Means to Love Yourself | Psychology Today, October 17, 2015. https://www.psychologytoday.com/us/blog/intimacy-path-toward-spirituality/201510/what-it-really-means-love-yourself.

Cherry, Kendra. "What Is Self-Esteem?" Verywell Mind, November 7, 2022. https://www.verywellmind.com/what-is-self-esteem-2795868#:~:text=Self%2Desteem%20is%20your%20subjective,your%20overall%20quality%20of%20life.

Cirino, Erica. "6 Ways to Build Trust in Yourself." Healthline, July 20, 2018. https://www.healthline.com/health/trusting-yourself.

Daniels, Dharius. *Relational intelligence: The people skills you need for the life of purpose you want.* Grand Rapids, MI: Zondervan, 2020.

Das, Tapatrisha. "Feeling Rejected? Therapist Shares Tips to Navigate through It." Hindustan Times, July 15, 2023. https://www.hindustantimes.com/lifestyle/relationships/feeling-rejected-therapist-shares-tips-to-navigate-through-it-101689401053502.html.

Davis, Tchiki. "Strengths & Weaknesses: Definition, Meaning, and 50+ Examples." The Berkeley Well-Being Institute. Accessed December 5, 2023. https://www.berkeleywellbeing.com/strengths.html#:~:text=Strengths%20are%20defined%20as%20character,or%20not%20as%20well%20developed.

Dictator Definition and Meaning | Collins English Dictionary, 2010. https://www.collinsdictionary.com/dictionary/english/dictator.

Elliott, Ed. "What David Discovered after He Committed Adultery and Murder." Medium, September 26, 2018. https://medium.com/publishous/what-david-discovered-after-he-committed-adultery-and-murder-4de5396cda3.

Hartikainen, Rikhard. "The Battlefield of the Mind." Hungry Generation, April 17, 2023. https://hungrygen.com/the-battlefield-of-the-mind-2/.

Holland, Kimberly. "Positive Self-Talk: Benefits and Techniques." Healthline, June 27, 2020. https://www.healthline.com/health/positive-self-talk#takeaway.

Mead, Elaine. "Personal Strengths Defined (+ List of 92 Personal Strengths)." PositivePsychology.com, March 25, 2020. https://positivepsychology.com/what-are-your-strengths/#list.

New Living Translation. *Holy Bible.* Tyndale House Publishers, 2007. 1 John 1:9.

New Living Translation. *Holy Bible.* Tyndale House Publishers, 2007. 1 Pet: 2:6.

New Living Translation. *Holy Bible.* Tyndale House Publishers, 2007. Eph. 1:4.

New Living Translation. *Holy Bible.* Tyndale House Publishers, 2007. Eph. 2:10.

New Living Translation. *Holy Bible.* Tyndale House Publishers, 2007. Eph. 3:18-19.

New Living Translation. *Holy Bible.* Tyndale House Publishers, 2007. Gen. 1:26-27.

New Living Translation. *Holy Bible.* Tyndale House Publishers, 2007. Heb. 13:8.

References

New Living Translation. *Holy Bible.* Tyndale House Publishers, 2007. Jer. 1:5.

New Living Translation. *Holy Bible.* Tyndale House Publishers, 2007. John 1:12.

New Living Translation. *Holy Bible.* Tyndale House Publishers, 2007. John 3:16.

New Living Translation. *Holy Bible.* Tyndale House Publishers, 2007. Matt. 22:37-40.

New Living Translation. *Holy Bible.* Tyndale House Publishers, 2007. Ps. 27:10.

New Living Translation. *Holy Bible.* Tyndale House Publishers, 2007. Ps. 118:22.

New Living Translation. *Holy Bible.* Tyndale House Publishers, 2007. Ps. 139:13-16.

New Living Translation. *Holy Bible.* Tyndale House Publishers, 2007. Rom. 5:8.

New Living Translation. *Holy Bible.* Tyndale House Publishers, 2007. Rom. 8:35-39.

New Living Translation. *Holy Bible.* Tyndale House Publishers, 2007. Song of Sol. 4:7.

Scazzero, Peter. *Emotionally healthy spirituality: Unleash a revolution in your life in christ.* Grand Rapids, MI: Zondervan, 2006.

"Smart Goals Template." Creately. Accessed December 5, 2023. https://creately.com/diagram/example/jezagrxp3/smart-goals-template.

"Types of Abuse." Southwest Family Advocacy Center. Accessed December 4, 2023. https://www.swfac.org/

abuse#:~:text=Perpetrators%20often%20consist%20of%20family,all%20victims%20know%20their%20perpetrators.

Walton, Alice G. "6 Ways Social Media Affects Our Mental Health." Forbes, June 30, 2017. https://www.forbes.com/sites/alicegwalton/2017/06/30/a-run-down-of-social-medias-effects-on-our-mental-health/?sh=7ef999dd2e5a.

"Weakness Definition and Meaning | Collins Dnglish Dictionary." Collins English Dictionary, 2005. https://www.collinsdictionary.com/dictionary/english/weakness.

Zavada, Jack. "Profile of King David, Father of Solomon." Learn Religions, December 12, 2018. https://www.learnreligions.com/king-david-man-after-gods-heart-701169#:~:text=King%20David%20was%20a%20man,run%20from%20vengeful%20King%20Saul.

Printed in the USA
CPSIA information can be obtained
at www.ICGtesting.com
CBHW071533120724
11524CB00003B/16

9 781662 894831